Manual on Pregnancy, Labour and Puerperium

The Author

Mrs. Rafiqa Bashir is an eminent Nursing Teacher and is presently working as Senior Lecturer in the College of Nursing, Sher-e-Kashmir Institute of Medical Sciences, Srinagar, J&K. She possesses Basic B.Sc., Nursing from Post Graduate Institute of Medical Education and Research, Chandigarh, Punjab University and Post Graduation from RAK College of Nursing, University of Delhi, with specialization in Maternity (Obstetrics & Gynaecological Nursing). She has 26 years of teaching experience of Diploma A Grade Nursing and Graduate Nursing Students. She has organized and attended many training courses, workshops, seminars, conferences, refresher courses at State and National level. She has published about 30 research papers in various professional Nursing journals. She is a life member of TNAI (Trained Nurses Association of India), ISHA (Indian Society of Health Administrators), AA (Aids Action), NNF (National Neonatology Forum) etc. The author has also served in TNAI as SNA advisor and Secretary, TNAI State Branch for a long time. Above all, the author is the most popular Nursing teacher in nursing fraternity.

Manual on Pregnancy, Labour and Puerperium

By

(Mrs.) Rafiqa Bashir

Senior Lecturer

College of Nursing

Sher-e-Kashmir Institute of Medical Sciences, Soura

Srinagar – 190 001, Kashmir

2019

Daya Publishing House®

A Division of

Astral International (P) Ltd.

New Delhi - 110002

ISBN 978-81-7035-524-3 (PB)

Published by : **Daya Publishing House**®
A Division of
Astral International Pvt. Ltd.
– ISO 9001:20**15** Certified Company –
47**36**/23, Ansari Road, Darya Ganj
New Delhi-110 002
Ph. 011-43549197, 23278134
E-mail: info@astralint.com
Website: www.astralint.com

Printed at : **Replika Press Pvt. Ltd.**

Acknowledgement

With unlimited humility, praise and thanks to "Allah" the Almighty, the Merciful, the compassionate, who bestowed me with health and courage in writing this "Manual on Pregnancy, Labour and Puerperium" for my students.

I express my deep sense of gratitude to Dr. I.A. Bukhari, Professor Hospital Administration and Medical Superintendent, SKIMS, Srinagar for his valuable guidance and encouragement in preparing the Manual. I fail to find words to express my feelings of honour and respect to Dr. Imtiyaz Ali, Professor & Head, Department of Community Medicine, SKIMS, Srinagar for his valuable suggestions and guidance while working on this Manual.

I would also like to extend my heart felt thanks to my colleagues in general and Mrs. Tanveer Makhdoomi in particular for their co-operation, suggestions and guidance.

While working on this project, I had consulted a lot of literature like Books, Periodical, Reports, Manuals authored by experienced professionals and would also like to thank them all.

I am equally thankful to my family members who have all along co-operated and supported me in accomplishing this Manual.

Srinagar **Mrs. Rafiqa Bashir**

DR. SYED I.A. BUKHARI
M.B.B.S., M.D., P.G.D.H.H.S.A. (London)
Professor Hospital Administration
and Medical Superitendent

GOVT. OF JAMMU & KASHMIR
Sher-I-Kashmir Institute of Medical Sciences, Soura
Post Bag 27, Srinagar 190 011 (J&K), India
Phone: (O) 2400084, 2400343, 2400348, 2400883
(Extn. 2182), 2402337; (R) 2433102, 2433102;
(M) 0941900318
Fax: 0194-2402337; E-mail: iabukh@yahoo.com

Foreword

Since India is among those countries which have a very high maternal mortality rate. More than 100,000 women die each year due to pregnancy related cause. About 80 per cent of maternal deaths are due to direct causes like obstetric complications of pregnancy, labour and puerperium or incorrect management. The maternal mortality rate can be significantly reduced by applying obstetric knowledge through antenatal, intranal and post-natal services. I hope the manual on pregnancy, labour and puerperium prepared by Mrs. Rafiqa Bashir, Sr. Lecturer, College of Nursing will act as a guide to nursing students, clinical instructors and for those health care workers who practice midwifery in various health care setting in order to provide care to pregnant women and their children to reduce the maternal and infant mortality rate.

Syed I.A. Bukhari
Medical Superintendent

Contents

Introduction

Being constantly insisted and hard pressed by my beloved students, I ultimately decided to write a compact, practically oriented "Manual on Pregnancy, Labour and Puerperium". It is an attempt to facilitate students with a comparatively easy technique of care to woman during labour and puerperium. This manual is written in, simple, clear and concise language with informative tables and illustrations. Although this manual is a combination of ideas, materials and my work experience as a Nurse Educator while teaching Maternal Nursing and Midwifery to Diploma and graduate students. There are twenty units and main emphasis is given on the subject, terminology, home care, care aspect during pregnancy, various stages of labour postnatal and postpartum period.

I sincerely hope that this manual will be of great help not only to my students but also to midwifery teachers for study as well as for reference and also to practicing midwives in various health care settings.

Mrs. Rafiqa Bashir
Sr. Lecturer
College of Nursing
SKIMS, Srinagar

Chpater 1

Normal Pregnancy

LEARNING OBJECTIVES

1. Define the terms listed
2. Explain the physiological adaptation to pregnancy
3. Identify major effects on pregnancy
4. Differentiate among presumptive, probable and positive sign of pregnancy.

Terminology

An understanding of the following terms used to describe the pregnant woman is essential to the study of maternity care.

Pregnancy

Is a state of carrying foetus inside uterus by a woman from conception to birth.

Gestation

Means pregnancy

Gestational Age

Is the duration of gestation from first day of normal menstrual period expressed in completed weeks.

Trimester of Pregnancy

3 months period

First Trimester

Is 12 weeks period from first day of last menstrual period

Second Trimester

Is from 13 to 28 weeks of pregnancy.

Third Trimester

Is from 29 to 40 weeks

Natal

Means birth

Antenatal/Prenatal

Means before birth

Intranatal

Means during birth

Postnatal

Means after birth

Gravida

A woman who is pregnant

Para

Refers to a woman who has given birth to a fetus at or after the age of viability i.e 28 weeks

Primi Garavida

A woman who is pregnant for the first time.

Multigravida

A woman who had two or more pregnancies

Grande Multigravida

A woman who has more than 4 viable births.

Nulligravida

A woman who has never been pregnant.

Primipara

A woman who has delivered once of a fetus or fetuses at or after the age of viability (28 weeks of pregnancy).

Multipara

A woman who delivered more than one fetus or fetuses at or after the age of viability.

Nullipara

A woman who has not given birth to foetus at or after the age of viability.

Viability

Capacity to live outside the uterus.

Birth

Complete expulsion from its mother of a foctus weighting 500 gm or more whether or not umbilical card has been cut or the placenta is attached.

Embryo

Is early foetus up to 10 weeks of pregnancy.

Foetus

Is intrauterine baby when pregnancy is 11 to 40 weeks.

Term

Is pregnancy from 37 completed weeks to less than 42 completed weeks (259 to 293 days).

Preterm

Is pregnancy from 28 to less than 37 completed weeks (less than 259 days).

Post Term

Is pregnancy of 42 completed weeks or more 294 days.

Chapter 2

Physiological Changes During Pregnancy

All physiological changes in the mother's body during pregnancy are due to the effects of specific hormones. (Case & Waterhouse 1940). These changes enable her to nurture the fetus, prepare her body for labour, develop her breasts for the production of breast milk during the puerperium.

Physiological Changes in the Reproductive System

The changes in pregnancy that take place in the reproductive system are temporary adaptation to meet the needs and demands of the fetus.

Ovaries

The ovaries are raised out of the pelvis as the uterus enlarges. The carpus luteum becomes greatly enlarged during early pregnancy under the effect of chorionic gonadotrophin. It produces oestrogen and progesterone. After 12 weeks the corpus luteum regresses, its hormonal activity is reduced and the placenta takes over its hormone secreting function until term.

The Body of Uterus

There is increase in growth and enlargement of the body of uterus in order to provide a nutritive and protective environment in which the fetus will develop and grow.

Decidua

Decidua is the name given to the endometrium during pregnancy. Under the effect of oestrogen and progesterone, the decidua becomes thicker and more vascular at the site of implantation. The decidua provide glycogen for the blastocyst until the placenta is formed and is able to produce its hormones.

Myometrium

The muscle fibers of the uterus continue to increase in size (hypertrophy) and in number (hyperplasia) for the first 20 weeks under the effect of oestrogen. After this time the uterus stretches under the effect of progesterone which encourages relaxation of smooth muscle.

The uterus at term increases in weight from 60 g to 900 g and in size from 7.5x5x2.5 cm to 30x23x20 cm and individual muscle cell grows 17 to 40 times (Verrals 1993). At 8 weeks gestation the uterus generates small waves of contraction known as Braxton Hicks Contractions. They are usually painless, last approximately 60 seconds and continue through out pregnancy.

Perimetrium

This is a layer of peritoneum. It does not cover the uterus being deflected over the bladder anteriorly to form the utero vesical pouch and over the rectum posteriorly to form the pouch of Douglas. This arrangement allows for the unrestricted growth of the uterus.

Endometrium

Formation of decidua. The increased structural and secretary activity of the endometrium that is brought about in response to progesterone following implantation is known as decidual reaction. The isthmus hypertrophies and elongates to about 3 times its original length. The circulatory arranged muscle fibers in the region function as sphincter in early pregnancy and thus helps to retain the fetus within the uterus.

Blood Supply

The blood supply to the uterus increase to meet the needs of all its growth and to meet the needs of placenta. New blood vessels are developed under the effect of oestrogen. The blood supply increases to about 750 ml per minute at term.

Changes in Uterine Shape

The uterus changes to globular shape in early pregnancy to anticipate fetal growth and also to accommodate increasing amounts of liquior and placental tissue.

1. At 12 weeks of pregnancy the uterus rises out of the pelvis and is no longer anteverted and ante flexed but becomes upright. This is known as right obliquity of the uterus.

2. At 20 weeks the uterus restores its original pear shape.
3. At 30 weeks the lower uterine segment can be identified.
4. At 36 weeks, the uterus reaches the level of xi phisternum.

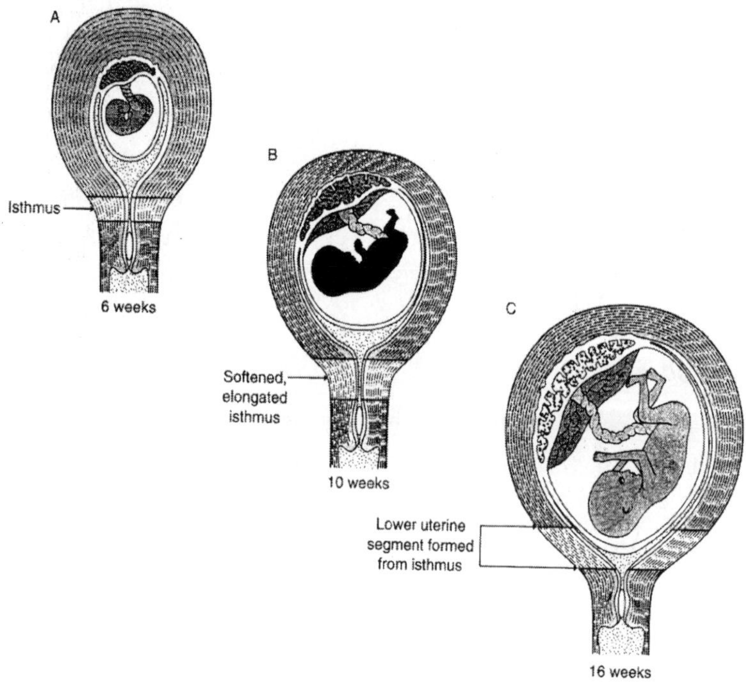

Changes in the Uterine Shape Between 6-16 weeks

(a) Uterine shape oval–6 (weeks);
(b) Uterus global–(10 weeks);
(c) Isthmus open to form lower segment–(16 weeks)

The Cervix

Under the influence of progesterone endocervical cells secrete mucus which becomes thicker and more viscous during pregnancy. This mucus forms a cervical plug called the operculum which provides protection from ascending infection. The cervix remains 2.5 cm long through out pregnancy.

In late pregnancy softening of the cervix occur in response to increasing painless contractions. Prostraglandins released from local tissue also play in cervical softening in readiness for one set of labour.

The Vagina

Oestrogen causes changes in the muscle layer and the mucosa of the vagina. The muscle layer hypertophies. Vagina becomes more elastic.

1. These changes enable it to dilate during the second stage of labour and receive the descending foetal head.
2. Changes in the mucosal increase the amount of white vaginal discharge (Leucorrhoea).
3. The mucosal cells have an increased glycogen content and interect with Doderleins bacillus to produce a more acid environment so as to provide an extra protection against infection.
4. Vagina is more vascular appearing reddish purple in colour.

Fallopian Tubes

The fallopian tubes on either side stretched out in pregnancy and is much more vascular.

Changes in Cardiovascular System

Profound changes takes place in the cardiovascular system during pregnancy and on understanding of these is important in the care of women with normal pregnancies as well as for the management of women with pre-existing cardiovascular disease.

Heart

The heart may increase in size due to increase in workload.

1. It may be displaced upwards and to the left, rotating anteriorly because of the increasing pressure from the growing uterus.
2. Cardiac output increases from 5 to 7 liters per minute by late pregnancy due to increase in blood volume.

The Blood Volume

Increased blood volume in pregnancy varies according to the size of the woman, the number of pregnancies and her parity and gravida.

1. The red cell mass (which is defined as the total volume of red cells in the circulation) increases 18 per cent in response to the extra oxygen requirement of maternal and placental tissues by the end of pregnancy.
2. The total amount of haemoglobin increased during pregnancy.
3. Plasma volume increases to 50 per cent by the end of 32-34th week.
4. This increase causes haemodilution effect which is characterized by lower Hb level (11-12g/dl blood), haematocrit and red cell count.

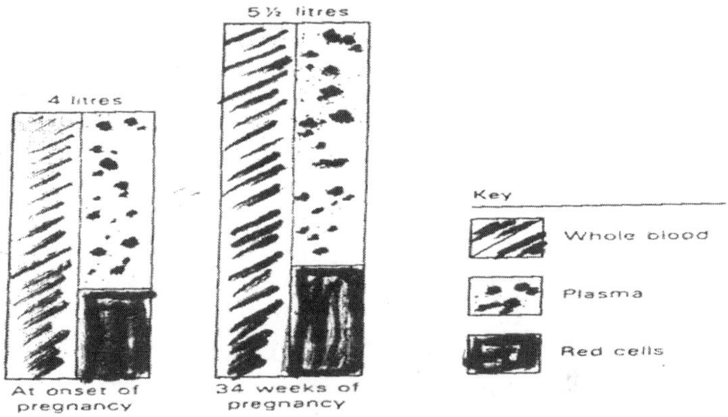

Changes in the Blood During Pregnancy

Iron Absorption

Iron requirement increases significantly in the last trimester, during which time iron absorption from gut is enhanced in order to prevent iron deficiency in the mother and of greatest fetal need.

Plasm Proteins

1. Increase during pregnancy.
2. Haemodilution effect causes a fall in albumin concentration and osmotic pressure as a result moderate physiological oedema is seen.
3. During 20 weeks of pregnancy, the plasma protein concentration is reduced 35 to 25 g/l from 65-85 g/L in non pregnancy.

Clotting Factor

Clotting factors are increased leading to a change of coagulation time from 12 to 8 minutes.

1. Capacity for clothing is increased and results in higher risk of thrombosis, embolism and prevention of hemorrhage at placental separation.

White Blood Cells

Are slightly increased especially neutrophils which enhances the blood's phagocytic and bacterial properties. These reach to the level of 10.0-15.0x10^9/L.

1. Levels of immunoglobulins decrease due to effect of haemodilution.

Blood Pressure

1. Remains the same or drops slightly in the first trimester, reaches its lowest level in mid trimester and towards term will return to the level of first trimester.
2. The pressure of gravid uterus compresses the vena cave reducing venous return this leads to reduced cardiac out put which gives rise to feeling of faintness and paraesthesia of the fingers (supine hypotensive syndrome).
3. In later pregnancy woman should avoid unsupported supine position as it causes profound hypotension.
4. Poor venous return in late pregnancy along with great distensability and pressure in the veins of the legs, vulva, rectum, pelvis can lead to hemorrhoids and varicose veins.
5. Maternal shock will participate fetal heart rate changes.

Blood Flow

1. Majority of blood flow is directed to the uterus, 80 per cent goes to the placenta.
2. Blood flow to kidney is increased by 30-50 per cent enhancing excretion.
3. Increased blood flow to skin eliminates extra heat.

Physiological Changes in the Respiratory System

1. The respiratory rate does not alter but the amount of air exhaled per minute increases from 7 to 11 liters.
2. The shape of chest changes and the circumferences increases in pregnancy by 6 cm.
3. Pregnant woman often become conscious of a need to breathe.
4. Nasal congestion occurs during pregnancy due to increased vascularity.
5. In later pregnancy the ribs flare out to counteract the pressure effect of the enlarged uterus upon the diaphragm.
6. The respiratory Mucosa becomes hyperemic and edematous with hyper secretion mucus leading to stiffness and epistaxis.

Changes in Gastrointestinal System

1. Nausea and vomiting occur during early pregnancy due to raised oestrogen or HcG levels.
2. Increased Salivation (Ptyalism) is common changes in the sense of taste lead to dietary changes and food craving.

3. Craving for unusual substances such as coal, mud and wall plaster is known as PiCa.
4. Oestrogen makes the gums spongy and leads to bleeding.
5. Dental problems occurs because of gingivitis.
6. Heart burn is associated with relaxing gastric reflex due to the effect of progesterone's action on the cardiac sphincter.
7. Constipation is a result of sluggish gut mobility. It can exacerbate hemorrhoids due to the relaxing effect of progesterone's action on the smooth muscle of the vein wall.
8. Increase in thirst due to fall in plasma polarity and rising levels of prolactin.

Changes in the Skin

1. Increased activity of the melanin stimulating hormone causes deeper pigmentation during pregnancy.
2. Choloasma is a deeper patchy coloring on the face which resumbles a mask also called mask of pregnancy.
3. Linea nigra is a pigmented line running from the pubis to the umbilicus.
4. The deposition of melanin toughens the nipple area and darkens the perineum.
5. Striae gravidarum are the stretch marks that appear as red stripes on the breasts abdomen and thighs.

6. A rise in body temperature of 0.5 degree C with an increase in blood supply causing vasodilatation leading to sweating.
7. Women feels hotter because of progesterone effect and vasodilatation

Changes in Skeletal System

1. Progesterone and relaxin encourages relaxation of ligaments and muscles.
2. The symphysis pubis and sacroiliac joints soften. The sacrococcygeal joints loosen to allow the coccyx to be displaced backwards.
3. Unstable pelvic joints result in rolling gait, backache and ligament pain.
4. The gravid uterus pulls the body forward, the woman leans backwards in order to balance and exaggerates the normal lumber curve (Lordosis)

Changes in Maternal Weight

The approximate weight gains during pregnancy is 12.5 Kg.

1. 4.0 kg in first 20 weeks
2. 8.5 kg in second 20 weeks (0.4 kg per week in the last trimester)
3. The average weight gain in multigravida is approximately 1 kg less than in primigravida.

Changes in Endocrine System

Placental Hormones

1. Placental hormones causes a number of physiological changes aiding in diagnoses of pregnancy.

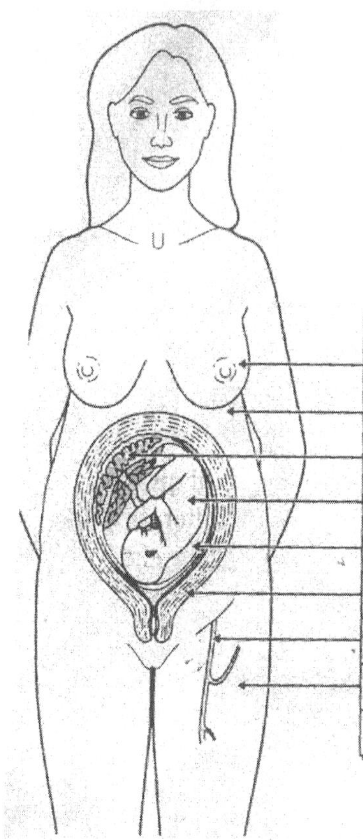

	kg
Breasts	0.4
Fat	3.5
Placenta	0.6
Fetus	3.4
Amniotic fluid	0.6
Uterus (increase)	1.0
Blood vol. (increase)	1.5
Extracellular fluid	1.5
Total	12.5

Weight Gain in Pregnancy

2. High levels of oestrogen and progesterone are responsible for breast changes, skin pigmentation and uterine enlargement.
3. The secretion of HPL(Human Placental Lactogen) and HCG (Human Chorconic Gonadotrophin) by the fetoplacental unit alters the mothers endocrine organs during pregnancy.

4. Human chorionic gonadotrophin (HCG) produced by cytotrophoblastic layer forms the basis of pregnancy tests.

Pituitary Hormones

1. The anterior pituitary gland increases by 30.50 per cent and the activities of Adreno carticotrophic hormone, melanocyte stimulating hormone, and thyrotrophic hormone.
2. Follicle stimulating hormone and leutiniseng hormone secretion are inhibited by progesterone and oestrogen
3. Prolactin secretions are suppressed during pregnancy but following delivery of placenta it stimulates milk production.
4. The posterior pituitary gland releases oxytocin but at term the frequency increases to stimulate uterine contractions.

Thyroid Hormones

1. Thyroid gland increases in size by about 13 per cent due to hyperplacia of glandular tissue and increased vascularity.
2. There is increased uptake of iodine leading to reduced level of plasma iodine.
3. The basal metabolic rate is increased because of increased oxygen consumption by the fetus.

Adrenal Hormones

1. Increased levels of plasma cortisol and cortricosteroids from 12th week to term.

2. The level of glucose in the blood is raised as made available to the fetus.
3. Raised levels of glucose in blood mobilises maternal fatty acids and amino acids and decreases the uptake of glucose by muscle and fat.
4. Increase in concentration of rennin in the first 12 weeks of pregnancy is due to stimulation of progesterone and oestrogen.

Changes in Breast

1. All breast changes are due to increased hormone activity.
2. Oestrogen develops the duct system and progesterone the glandular tissue.
3. Prolaction stimulates the production of colostrum.
4. The breasts enlarge due to increased tissue growth, blood supply and fat deposition.

Change in Urinary System

1. Renal blood flow increases by 70-80 per cent by the second trimester and decreases slowly after 30 weeks.
2. The kidneys enlarge and glomerular filtration increases.
3. Plasma levels of urea, uric acid and creatinin fall and uric acid level returns to normal in late pregnancy.
4. Protein and amino acids are less efficiently reabsorbed and as a result found in greater amount in the urine.

5. Glycosuria is quite common as glucose excretion increases.
6. Urinary output decreased because of enhanced tubular reabsorption of water.
7. Urine is alkaline due to alkalemea of pregnancy and increased production of urine causes frequency of micturation in early pregnancy but in later pregnancy it is due to the pressure of gravid uterus on the bladder.
8. The ureters become dilated relaxed due to influence of progesterone and the bladder muscles also become relaxed.
9. Bladder vascularity increases and bladder capacity is reduced.
10. The entire bladder becomes displaced upwards due to engaged head at the end of pregnancy.

Changes in Metabolism

1. There is increased diatory intake of approximately 200-300 Kcal per day.
2. The alteration in the metabolism of carbophydrates, proteins and fats due to human placental lactogen to ensure glucose is readily available for the developing fetus and protect nutritional deficiencies.
3. Fasting plasma glucose concentration falls during first trimester but rises between 16 and 32 weeks then falls towards term.
4. Fasting in pregnancy produces intense ketosis (known as accelerated starvation) and hypoglycemia.

5. Plasma albumin concentration is reduced due to increased plasma volume causing reduction of colloid osmotic pressure leading to limb edema.
6. Plasma calcium concentration fall as a result of fetal needs and haemodilation. Therefore calcium intake by 70 per cent should be increased
7. Fat is stored during pregnancy from glucose for future lactation.
8. Calcium intake in food is doubled to 1000 mg to meet extra demands during pregnancy.

Chapter 3

Diagnosis of Pregnancy

Learning Objectives

The learners will be able to:

1. List signs of pregnancy
2. Explain the changes evident in the mother
3. Diagnose pregnancy at different stages of gestation
4. Explain the different pregnancy tests

DIAGNOSIS OF PREGNANCY

Pregnancy occurs during reproductive period (15-44 yrs). Pregnancy spans is 9 (nine) calendar months, 10 lunar months or approximately 40 weeks. Average duration of pregnancy is 280 days from the first day of last menstrual period. Pregnancy may be diagnosed by the woman herself even before she has missed a period because she feels different and changes in the breast occur as early as 5-6 weeks after conception.

Pregnancy is divided in to

1. Early pregnancy first trimester from I^{st}. to 12th weeks (total 12 weeks)
2. Mid pregnancy/second trimester from 13th-27th week (total-15 weeks)
3. Late pregnancy/third trimester from 28th-40th week (total 13 weeks)
4. Diagnosis of pregnancy in the first and early second trimester is based on a combination of presumptive and probable signs of pregnancy.

Signs and Symptoms of Pregnancy

There are three classifications of clinically diagnosing pregnancy by many signs and symptoms.

The Presumptive (Possible) Signs and Symptoms

These are the maternal physiological changes, which the woman experiences and in most cases indicate that she is pregnant these are:

Amenorrhoea

(Missing of Menses) Abrupt cessation of menstruation at 4th week. It is an early indication for a woman with regular cycle.

Morning Sickness

Nausea and vomiting occur mainly in the morning from 14th week. Changes in food and drink preference may also occur. Raised level of placental human chorionic gonadotrophin and emotional factor are held responsible cause.

Breast Changes

Breast changes in chronological order

Weeks of Gestation	*Changes*
3-4 weeks	Prickling, tingling sensation due to increased blood supply particularly around nipple
6 weeks	Developing ducts and glands cause the breasts to be enlarged, painful and tense
8 weeks	Bluish surface veins are visible
8-12 weeks	– Montgomery's tubercles become more prominent on the areola.
	– These sebaceous glands secrete sebum which keeps the nipple soft and supple.
	– The pigmented area around the nipple darkens and may enlarge slightly and this area is known as primary areola.
16 weeks	– Colostrums can be expressed.
	– Further extension of the pigmented area occurs and is often mottled in appearance called secondary areola.
Late pregnancy	– Colostrums may leak from the breasts.
	– Progesterone causes the nipple to become more prominent and mobile.

Skin Changes

Skin changes such as chloasma, linea nigra and stria gravida, Pigmentation and palmor erythema.

Frequency of Micturation

(Bladder irritability) occurs around 6th to 12th weeks is caused by the pressure of the enlarging uterus on the bladder.

Quickening

The date of the first fetal movements felt by the mother can be used to check the expected date of delivery. Aprimigravida woman feels it at 18-20 weeks while multigravida feels it at 16-18 weeks.

Fatigue

Particularly in early pregnancy and due to backache.

Probable Signs and Symptoms

These are the maternal physiological changes other than presumptive signs, which are detected upon examination and documented by examiner these are:

Jacquemier's Sign/Chadwicks Sign

Is a voilet blue discoloration of the vaginal membrane due to increased vascularity (8th week+).

Osianders Sign

Is an increased pulsation felt in the lateral vaginal fornices (8th week).

Hegar's Sign

Is the softness of the elongated isthmus marked between the 6th and 12th week of pregnancy.

Uterine Growth

After 12th week of gestation, the uterus can be felt through the abdominal wall just above the symphysis pubis.

Braxton Hicks Contractions

Are painless contractions of the uterus occurring at irregular intervals during pregnancy felt from (16th week).

Ballotment of Fetus

Is a sinking and rebounding of the fetus in amniotic fluid in response to sudden tap on the uterus. It occurs between 16th and 28th weeks of pregnancy.

Uterine Suffle

Is a soft blowing sound heard on auscultation from 16th weeks onward. It is due to blood passing through the uterine arteries of the mother particularly over the placental site. It is synchronous with the mothers pulse.

Positive Signs

Are those directly attributable to the fetus as detected and documented by the examiner. These signs are:

1. Visualization of fetus by ultrasound 6th week +.
2. Visualization of fetal skeleton by X-ray (16th weeks).
3. Fetal heart sounds by ultrasound (6th week)
4. Fetal heart sounds with fetoscope (20th week)
5. Palpable fetal movements (22 weeks)
6. Visible fetal movements
7. Palpation of fetal parts (24 week +).

Chapter 4

Clinical Diagnosis of Pregnancy

The early signs and symptoms of pregnancy:

Pregnancy Tests

Positive hormonal tests for pregnancy produced by presence of human chorionic gonadotrophin hormone in maternal blood and urine after implantation.

Abdominal Palpation

The pregnant uterus is palpable just above the symphysis pubis at about 12 weeks. Palpation of fetal movement at 22 weeks and fetal parts at 24 weeks.

Vaginal Examination

There are general changes in the vagina and cervix.

Fetal Movements

Woman having a first baby usually feel the first fetal movements (quickening) at 20 weeks.

Auscultation of fetal heart rate.

Abdominal Enlargement.

Chapter 5

Estimated Date of Birth

Estimated date of birth has traditionally been termed as the estimated date of confinement (EDC) but estimated date of delivery (EDD) or expected date of birth (EDB) is usually used.

Many formulas or rules of thumb have been suggested for the calculation of EDB but Naegles's rule is common, reasonably accurate and usually used.

Naegle's Rule

Add 7 days to the first day of the LMP and count forward 9 month or subtract 3 month and add one year. For example if the first day of LMP was July 10, 1994 the EDB is April 17, 1995 or Add 7 days to the LMP and count forward 9 months.

Other Methods

1. Patient's statement like date of fruitful coitus and date of quickening.

2. Clinical like size of uterus, palpation of fetal parts and auscultation of FHR.
3. Investigation records like positive pregnancy testes, ultrasonograhpic findings.

Estimation of Fetal Height

1 Height of uterus and growth of abdomen are measured at the level of umbilicus.
2. Size of head, hardening of skull bones and amount of liquor amnii as felt per abdomen.

Using Johnson's Formula

The height of uterus above the symphysis pubis in centimetres minus 12, multiplied by 155 e.g (32-12)x155=3100gm. This is used in vertex presentation.

Sonography: Measurement of fetal abdominal circumstance at the level of umbilical vein, femur length and biparietal diameter together gives accuracy.

Chapter 6
Antenatal Care

Introduction

The pregnancy period is a preparatory one both physically, in terms of fetal growth and maternal adaptation and psychologically in terms of anticipation of parenthood. Becoming a parent represents one of the maturational crises of our lives and as such can represent a time of intense learning for the parents. It aims to provide appropriate support for the woman and her family regarding the outcome of pregnancy.

This Chapter aims at:

1. Discuss the initial assessment visit, defining objectives and components of the history;
2. Describe the physical examination of the woman during the initial and subsequent visits;

3. Details the methods of abdominal examination to check the growth of the fetus, its position and heart rate;
4. Enumerate the nursing care during antenatal period and health education to pregnant mother.

ANTENATAL CARE

Antenatal care refers to the care given to an expected mother from the time of confirmed conception until the beginning of labour.

Objectives

1. Promote, protect and maintain the health of the mother during pregnancy
2. Recognize deviation form normal and provide management of treatment as required
3. Remove anxiety and fear associated with pregnancy
4. Reduce maternal and infant morbidity and mortality
5. Teach the mother nutrition, personal hygiene and newborn care.
6. Explain the mother the need of family planning.

Antenatal Visits

Ideally the antenatal mother should visit the antenatal clinic once a month during first seven months, twice a month during eighth month and once a week there after if everything is normal. If pregnancy is uncomplicated, a minimum of three visits covering the entire period of pregnancy (as outlined in park 2000).

1. 1st visit at 20 weeks or as soon as pregnancy is known
2. 2nd visit at 32nd week
3. 3rd visit at 36th week

Assessment of Maternal and Fetal Wellbeing. It includes:

History Taking

Social History

1. This gives a picture of the woman as an individual and provides a helpful indication of any problem if she have.
2. Personal details are recorded name, address, age. Marital status, occupation of woman and her husband
3. Environmental factors, poor living conditions, low socio economics status
4. Religion beliefs or practices associated with child birth and life style, dietary taboos.
5. Nationality and language also recorded.

Medical History

1. Pervious hospital admissions, childhood illnesses, serious illnesses, medical problems, known allergy or sensitivity.
2. Details of surgery especially on genital tract
3. Accidents involving bony injury to the pelvis
4. Any blood transfusion

Family History

1. Genetic diseases in the baby is much more likely to occur if parents are close relatives such as first cousins
2. Prevalence of diabetes, hypertension, multiple pregnancies, cardiac diseases, congenital

abnormalities and allergic conditions such as asthma within the family.

3. Conditions like sickle cell anaemia, thalassaemia
4. Poor living conditions may result in tuberculoses, vitamin deficiency causing spina bifida.

Menstrual History

1. Age at Menarche
2. Frequency, duration and amount of menstrual flow.
3. Dys functional uterine bleeding
4. Pre-menstrual spotting
5. Any treatment for menstrual problem/infertility

Obstetric History

1. Obtaining the data of her last menstrual period (LMP)
2. Calculation of her expected date of delivery (EDD)
3. Calculation of her gravida and para status.
4. Rh and ABC blood type
5. Previous pregnancy and delivery
6. Weeks of gestation and date of termination.
7. Type of delivery i.e instrumental, spontaneous or casessarian section.
8. Status of newborn at birth

Physical Examination

General examination should be done systematically, start by looking at the women's face and then progress downward to finish with legs and feet.

General Appearance

1. The health of the woman can be assessed by looking at her face.
2. The hair of a healthy woman is shinning and glossy.
3. Her eyes are bright and clear
4. Her general manner indicates vigour and vitality.
5. Woman, who is anaemic, depressed tired or ill appears lethargic, is not interested in her appearance, unenthusiastic about the interview.
6. Any signs of ill health should be reported.

Height

Height of the woman is checked at the time of first visit, height over 160 cm and shoe size above 3 indicates normal pelvis.

Weight

Weight must be checked at every visit and rate of weight gain is assessed. Obesity is associated with an increased risk of gestational diabetes and pregnancy induced hypertension.

Blood Pressure

Blood pressure is taken to ascertain normality and provide a baseline reading for comparison through out pregnancy. A blood pressure of 140/90 mm Hg at the first visit is indicative of hypertension

Breast Examination

1. The breast should be gently palpated to feel any lumps.
2. The nipple should be drawn forward to see if it is protractile

3. Breast changes due to pregnancy should be observed.

Elemination

Woman should be

1. Asked about her bowel habits
2. Routine urine analysis is carried at every visit
3. Frequency of micturation is common in early and late pregnancy
4. Hormonal changes may alter normal function in late pregnancy.

Vaginal Discharge

1. Vaginal discharge increases during pregnancy
2. If discharge is itchy, cause soreness and offensive, infection suspected and investigated.

Vaginal Bleeding

1. In early pregnancy spotting may occur at the time of menstruation.
2. Vaginal bleeding at any time during pregnancy should be reported.

Legs

1. Oedema should be noted, physiological oedema occurs after rising in the morning get worsens due to daily activities or hot weather
2. Pitting oedema in lower limb is tested by applying fingertip pressure for 10 seconds over the tibial bone.

3. Varicosities is more likely to occur during pregnancy and are predisposing cause of deep vein thrombosis
4. The woman should report tenderness during examination.

Blood Tests

1. ABO blood group and Rh factor.
2. Haemoglobin and heamatocrit
3. Venereal Disease Research Laboratory (VDRL) test.
4. Human Immuno deficiency virus (HIV) screening
5. Rubella immune status.

Abdominal Examination

1. Abdominal examination should be performed at every visit.
2. The uterus will be palpable abdominal after 12th week of gestation.

Aims

1. To observe signs of pregnancy
2. To assess fetal size and growth
3. To assess fetal health
4. Diagnose fetal parts
5. Detect any deviation
6. Abdominal examination includes:

Inspection

1. The size of the uterus
2. Shape of the uterus
3. Fetal movement
4. Skin changes

Palpation

Estimation of the period of gestation from fundal height.

Approximate Fundal Height at Various Weeks of Gestation

Weeks Gestation	*Approximate Location of Fundal Height*
12	Level of symphysis pubis
16	Half way between symphysis pubis and umbilicus
20	1-2 finger breadth below the umbilicus
22-24	Level of the umbilicus
28-30	3 fingers breadth above umbilicus
32	3-4 finger breadth below the xiphoid process
36	Level of the xiphoid process
40	2-3 finger breadth below the xiphoid process if lightning occurs

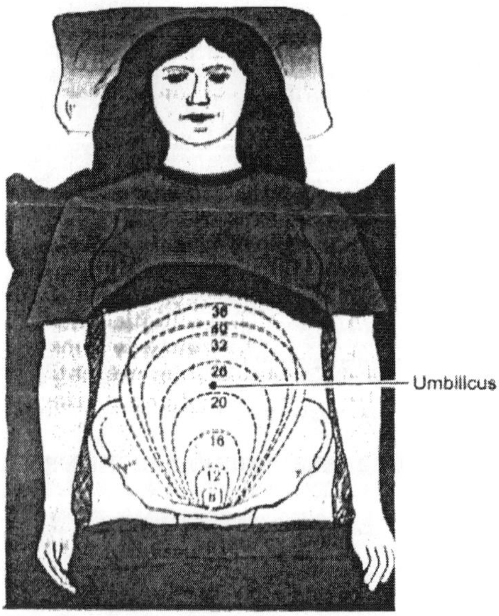

Approximate Expected Location of the Normal Height of the Fundus During Pregnancy

Attitude

Is the relationship of the fetal head and limbs to its trunk, the attitude should be flexion.

LIE

Is the relationship of the long axis of the fetus to the long axis of the uterus. There are three lies-longitudinal, transverse and oblique. In 99 per cent cases the lie is longitudinal, the remainder are oblique and transverse.

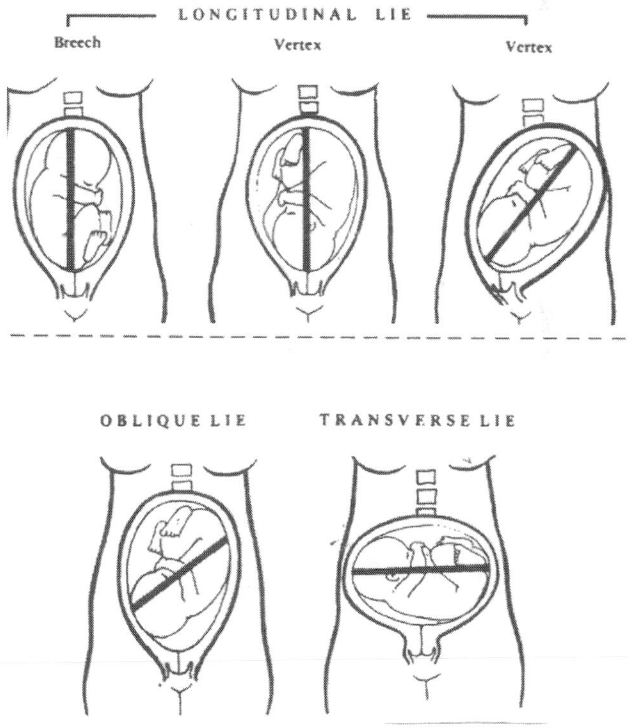

Presentation

It refers to the part of fetus which lies in the lower pole of the uterus there are three presentations cephatic, breech and shoulder the I[st]. two are further subdivided. Cephalic

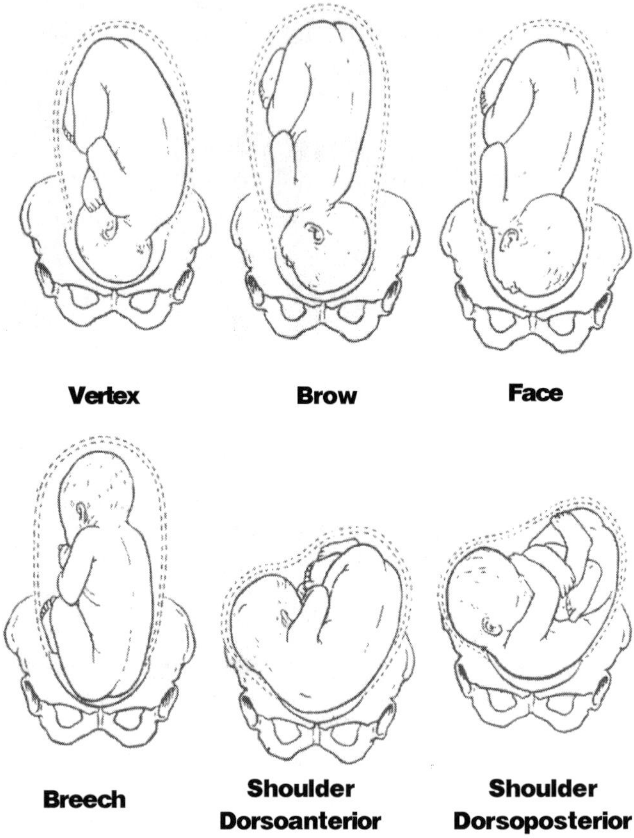

The Five Presentations

into vertex brow and face. When head is well flexed the vertex presents. In 96.8 per cent cases are in vertex presentation, when head is fully extended face presents, breech 2.5 per cent cases.

Denominator

Is the name of the part of the presentation that is when referring to the fetal position. Each presentation has different denominator.

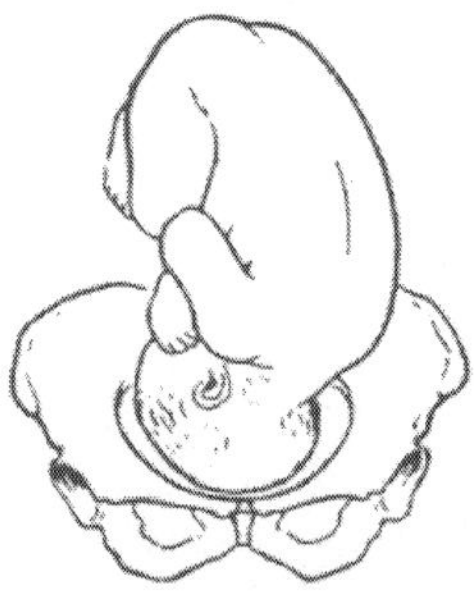

Left Occipotoanterior

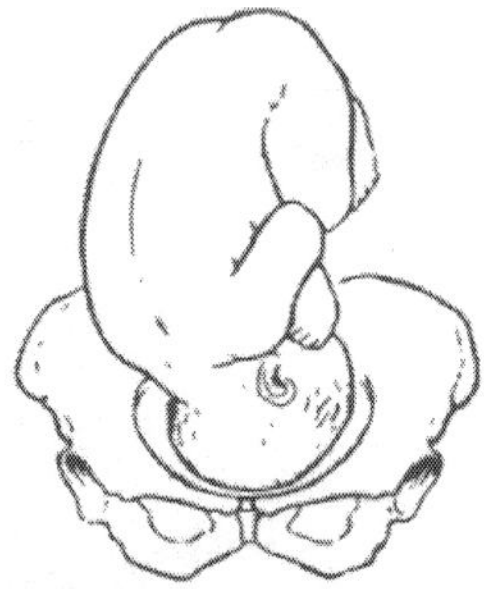

Right Occipotoanterior

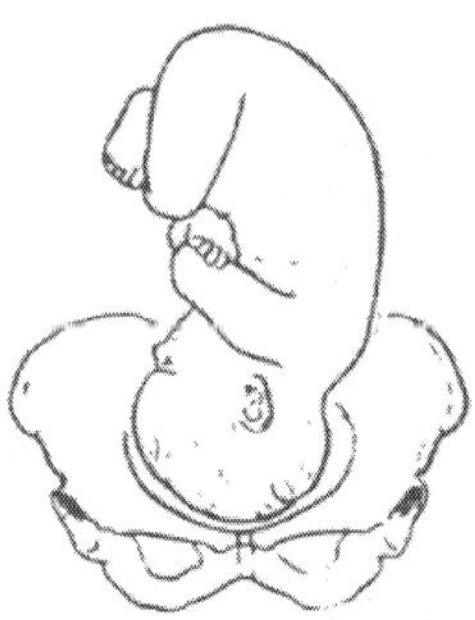

Left Occipitolateral

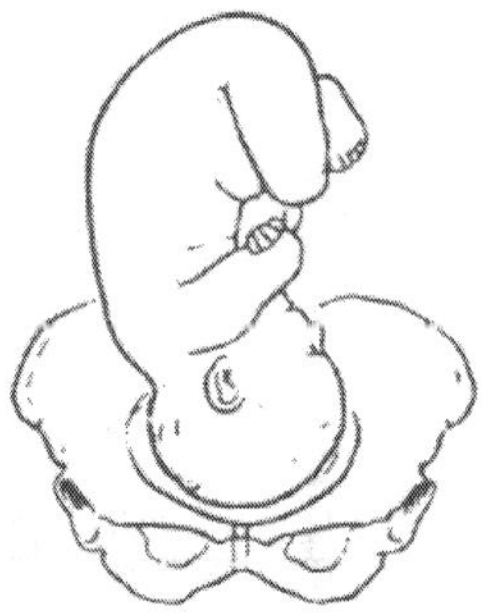

Right Occipitolateral

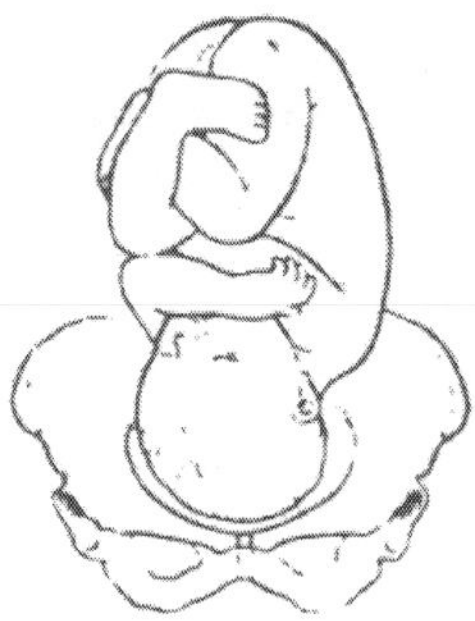

Left Occipitoposterior

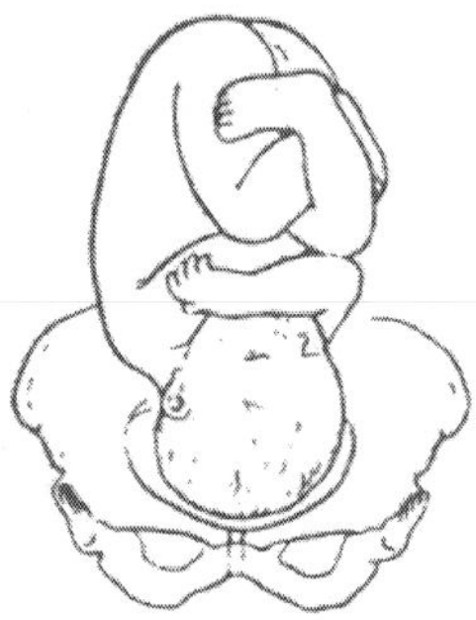

Right Occipitoposterior

In vertex presentation	-	Occiput is denominated
In breech presentation	-	Sacrum is denominated
In face presentation	-	Mentum is denominated
In shoulder presentation	-	Acromion process is denominator
In brow	-	No denominator

Position

Is the relationship between the denominator and six points in the pelvic brim.

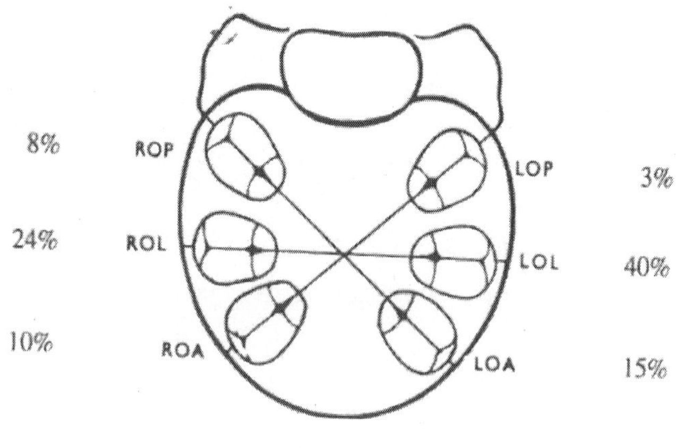

Diagrammatic Representation of the Six Vertex Positions and their Relative Frequency
LOA: Left occipitoanterior; LOL: Left occipitolateral; LOP: Left occipitoposterior; ROA: Right occipitoanterior; ROL: Right occipitolateral; ROP: Right occipitoposterior

Leopold's Manoeuvres

There are four manoeuvres Fundal, Lateral, Pawlikes and Pelvic

Fundal Palpation

It is carried out in order to determine whether it contains the breech or the head. This will help to diagnose the lie and presentation of fetus.

Lateral Palpation

Is used to locate the fetal back in order to determine position.

Pawliks Palpation

Is used to judge the size, flexion and mobility of the head.

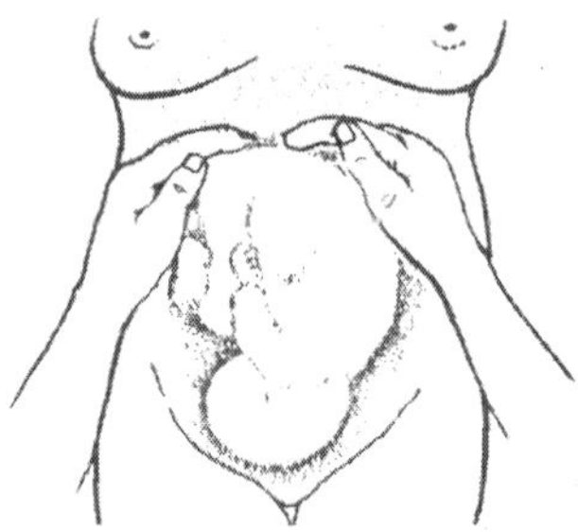

(A) First Manoeuvre (Fundal Palpation)

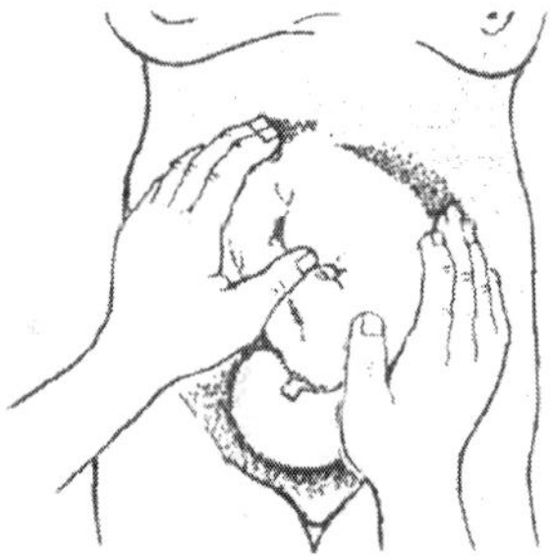

(B) Second Manoeuvre (Lateral Palpation)

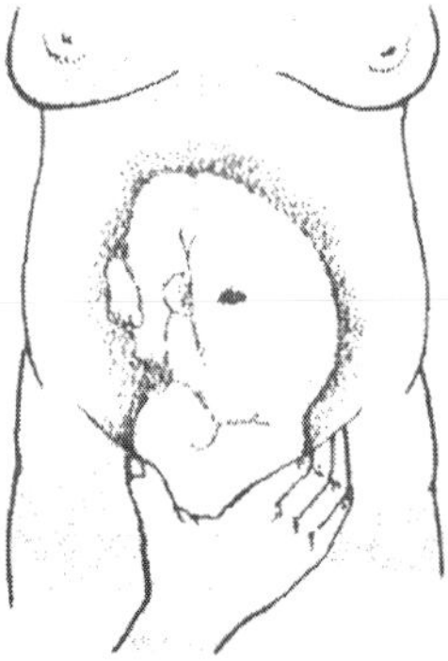

(C) Third Manoeuvre (Pawlik's Grip)

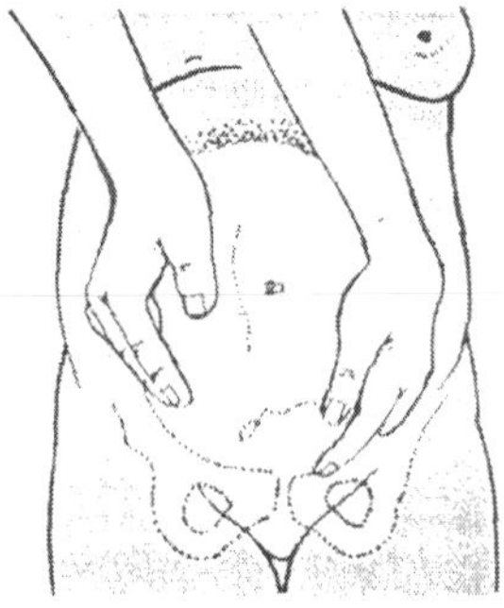

(D) Four Manoeuvre (Pelvic Palpation)

Pelvic Palpation

Is the palpation of lower uterus just above the pelvis. If the head is presenting, hard mass, with distinctive round smooth surface is felt.

Auscultation

The fetal heart is heard through the abdominal wall using a Stethoscope, Doppler and Cardiotocograph.

Dealing with Physical, Psychological and Life Style Changes

Rest

Adequate rest is important, advice regarding the use of extra pillows given to woman in late pregnancy to increase comfort and enable sleep. Swollen ankles may be relieved by sitting with the feet up and avoid prolong standing.

Hygiene

Perspiration and vaginal secretions increase during pregnancy so a daily all-over wash is necessary. General advice includes keeping the breasts clean and nipples free from encrusted colostrum.

Clothing

Loose cool clothing will be the most comfortable. Shoes need to be comfortable. A suitable well-fitted bra should be used in order to be comfortable and give support to the breasts.

Teeth

Dental decay may occur during pregnancy because of fetal demands for calcium

Travel

Airlines asks for doctor's certificate stating that a pregnant woman is fit to travel they prefer not to take ladies beyond 32nd week. Long unbroken journey should be avoided. If travel is essential, taking extra fluids and making breaks can ease any discomfort.

Alcohol and Smoking

Moderate to high levels of alcohol have been found to give rise to fetal problems. Alcohol consumption should be discontinued before and during pregnancy. Smoking causes intra uterine growth retardation, preterm labour and an increase in prenatal mortality rate. The mother is at increased risk of other infection and thrombo-embolic disorders.

Sexual Intercourse

Sexual intercourse is absolutely safe and normal unless specific problem exist. If a mother has a history of abortion she should avoid intercourse in the early months. After an episode of preterm labour intercourse should be avoided in the late months.

Drugs

Many drugs are known to have an adverse effect on pregnancy oral contraceptive pill should be discontinued 3 to 6 months before a woman tries to become pregnant. Medication of any kind should be avoided unless prescribed by doctor.

Infections

Any infection such as urinary, vaginal or respiratory tract or sexually transmitted diseases occurring in either partner should be treated.

Danger Signs of Pregnancy

Abnormal symptoms may be reported by the woman. Mother should be encouraged to report and seek advice if any of the following warning symptoms occur.

1. Vaginial bleeding
2. Persistent abdominal pain.
3. Reduce/stoppage of fetal movement.
4. Frontal or recurrent headaches
5. Sudden swelling of feet, finger and face.
6. Rupture of membranes
7. Vaginial discharge with itching or odour
8. Premature onset of contractions

Nutrition in Pregnancy

1. Adequate nutrition is important for the health of the woman, her developing fetus and the reduction of minor disorders of pregnancy.
2. The intake of protein is important for the growth of new tissue. Prime sources are meat, fish and cheese cheaper sources include peas, beans lentils, milk and eggs.
3. Calcium and iron are vital in pregnancy. Calcium is found in milk and eggs. Iron is found in red meat, green vegetables and red fruits.
4. Vitamin C helps the absorption of iron and is found in fresh fruits and vegetables.
5. Fiber content of the diet helps to prevent constipation.

6. A certain amount of carbohydrate is required to provide energy.
7. High sugar intake is recorded and starches are taken as they are absorbed more slowly.

Exercises

1. Regular exercise such as walking should be continued as long as mother feels comfortable.
2. Mother should not try out strenuous sports during pregnancy.
3. Figure changes during pregnancy put extra strain on joints and muscles, which cause discomfort.

Expected Outcome of Antenatal Care

Expected outcome to physiological care include the following:

1. Woman and her family will have pertinent information about maternal adaptations and fetal development as a basis for understanding the management of care during pregnancy.
2. Woman will finalize the birth plan.
3. Woman will demonstrate knowledge for self care.
4. Woman will use knowledge of nutritional needs, sexual needs, activities of daily living discomforts of pregnancy and self care.
5. Woman will recognize symptoms that indicate deviations from normal progress and knows protocols for reporting them.
6. Woman and their families will activity participate in their care during pregnancy.

Chapter 7

Minor Disorders in Pregnancy

Minor disorders of pregnancy are not life threatening, if treated promptly. They are caused by normal accommodation, Metabolic and postural changes.

Digestive System

Nausea and Vomiting

It is a common disorder seen in about 50 per cent women between 4 and 16 week of gestation. The most likely cause is hormonal influences such as human choronic gonadotrophin, oestrogen and progesterone. The sickness is not confined to early morning but can occur at any time in the day. Understanding the cause helps in coping. Salads and light snacks are more tolerable than full meals. Suggest small frequent feeds. Solid food may be tolerated better than liquid foods e.g. dry toast, biscuits, carbohydrate and snacks at bed time and before rising can prevent hypoglycaemia which causes nausea and vomiting.

Heart Burn

Is a burning sensation in the mediastinal region. Progesterone relaxes the cardiac sphincter of the stomach and allows reflux of gastric contents into the oesophagus. From about 30-40 weeks gestation, the pressure of the growing uterus on stomach also cause heart burn.

If the heart burn is occasional, the reflex can be prevented by avoiding bending over and lying flat. Small meals take up less room in the reduced stomach space and are digested more easily. Sleeping with more pillows and laying on the right side can sometimes help. For persistent heart burn, antiacids may be prescribed by the doctor.

Excessive Salivation (Ptyalism)

This occurs from 8 weeks gestation and is caused by the hormones of pregnancy. It may accompany heart burn. Explanation and attentive listening are helpful.

Pica

This is the term used when a mother craves certain foods or unnatural substances such as coal. The cause is unknown but may be due to hormones and changes in metabolism. If the craved substances are harmful to the fetus, the mother must be helped to take medical advice.

Constipation

Progesterone causes relaxation and decreased peristalsis of the gut which is also displaced by the growing uterus. Constipation is sometimes associated with the taking of oral iron. It is helpful to increase the intake of water, fresh fruits, vegetables and whole meal foods in the diet. A glass of warm water in the morning before tea or breakfast may activate the gut and help regular bowl movements. Walking exercises is helpful constipation is sometimes associated with taking oral iron.

Musculo Skeletal System

Backache

1. Backache may be due to increasing lordosis.
2. Advice mother to maintain posture.
3. The hormones sometimes soften the ligaments to such a degree that some support is needed.
4. The mother is reassured that once birth has occurred, the ligaments will return to their prepregnant strength.

Cramps

1. The cause is unknown. It may be due to ischemic or changes in the PH or electrolyte status.
2. To relieve sudden cramp in the calf muscle in the sitting position, woman may be advised to hold the knee straight and stretch the calf muscle by pulling the foot upward (dorsiflexion). Stand firmly on the affected leg.
3. Raise the foot of the bed about 25 cm.
4. Gentle leg movements whilst in a warm bath enhance circulation and removes waste products from muscle.
5. Vitamin B complex and calcium are the other remedies used.

Genito Urinary System

Frequency of Micturation

Occurs in early weeks of pregnancy due to the pressure of growing uterus on the bladder. In the later weeks, the head usually enters the pelvis and reduces the space required by the bladder.

1. The mother should be reassured that the problem is resolved when the uterus raises into the abdomen after the 12th week.

Leukorrhoea

This is the term used for the increased white, nonirritant vaginal discharge in pregnancy.

1. If the discharge is foul smelling or irritating medical advice is needed.
2. Simple advice on washing the perineal area with plain water twice a day.
3. The woman should wear cotton underwear and avoid tights.
4. Mild cream is preferable.

Circulatory System

Fainting

In early pregnancy fainting may be due to the vasodilatation effect of progesterone.

1. Avoiding long periods of standing reduces such attacks.
2. If woman feels slightly faint she should sit or lie on her left side.

3. Fainting in late pregnancy while lying flat on the back may be due to supine hypotensive syndrome this is because the weight of the uterine contents presses on the inferior venacava and slows the return of blood to the heart. Turning the mother quickly on to her left side will bring about rapid recovery.
4. Explain to the mother the reason and advice to avoid lying on the back.

Varicosities

1. Progesterone relaxes the smooth muscles of the veins and results in sluggish circulation. The values of dilated veins become inefficient and varicosities results.
2. Varicose veins may occur in the legs, anus (haemorrhoids) and vulva due to pelvic congestion.
3. Mothers at risk include those with a family history and those who regularly stand or sit for long periods.
4. Exercising the calf muscles by raising the toes or making circular movements with the ankles will help the venous return.
5. In early pregnancy, resting with the legs vertical against the wall for a short time will drain the veins.
6. Support tights should be put on before rising or after resting with leg elevated to increase comfort.
7. Exacerbation of haemorrhoids will be reduced by avoiding of constipation, local application and medical advice.

8. Avoid wearing half stocking and clothes that cost pressure on legs and thighs.
9. Vulval varicosities are rare and very painful. A panty girdle or sanitary pad may give support.
10. Vulval varicosities may rupture and bleed during delivery.

Skin

1. Generalized itching over the abdomen results from livers response to the pregnancy hormones and raised bilrubin levels.
2. Itching will be reduced after child birth
3. Local applications and antihistamins will provide comfort.

Nervous System

Carpal-tunnel Syndrome

1. The mother complains of numbness and pins and needles in the fingers and hands in the morning or at any time of the day.
2. It is caused by fluid retention which creates oedema and pressure on the median nerve.
3. Wearing a splint at night with hand resting high on two or three pillows sometimes gives relief.
4. This syndrome usually resolves spontaneously following delivery
5. Diuretics may be prescribed by the doctor
6. Restriction of salt intake is recommended.

Insomnia (Nocturnal Frequency)

1. Relatively common in late pregnancy owing to the discomfort caused by the fetal movements, frequency of micturation and difficulty in finding a comfortable position.
2. Going to bed earlier may give the baby an active period and allow the mother to sleep at her usual time.
3. Anxiety will be relieved by talking through common fears of pregnancy.
4. Sensitive listening, explanation and reassurance can be helpful.
5. Alie in the morning or a rest in the afternoon will help to prevent tiredness and depression that can occur in the last trimester of pregnancy.
6. Sharing the mothers feelings can result in a sense of normality and lightness.
7. Depression due to hormonal changes towards the end of pregnancy may be relieved by encouraging the woman to think about positive aspects of the baby and having a family life.

Chapter 8

Antenatal Exercises

The following exercises will help to lessen the strain and ensure a more comfortable pregnancy.

Purposes

1. To improve circulation in legs and help in the prevention of cramp, varicose veins and swollen feet and ankles, walking is important.
2. To improve the oxygen supply, sit or lie down comfortable, take a slow deep breath and then sigh the air out slowly.
3. To prevent and ease backache and strength tummy muscles.

Exercise-I: Abdominal Breathing

1. Lie on back with knees bent;
2. Inhale deeply through the nose, keeping ribs as stationary as possible and allowing the abdomen to expand up;
3. Exhale slowly but forcefully while contracting the abdominal muscles;
4. Hold for about 3 to 5 seconds while exhaling, relax;
5. Begin with 2 repetitions, gradually progressing to 10.

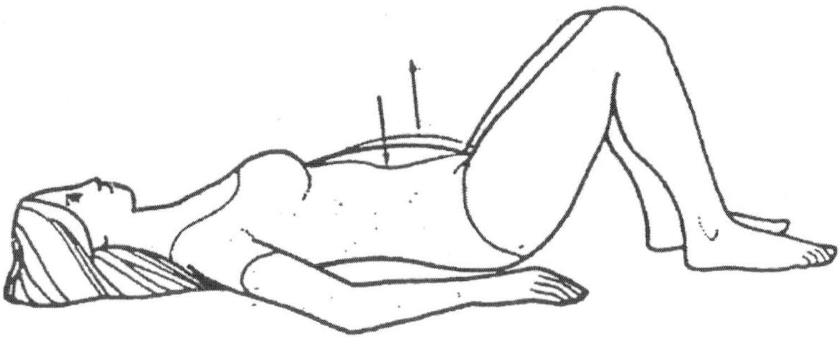

Exercise-II: Pelvic Tilting

1. Lie on back with knees bent and feet flat;
2. Lower both knees slowly to the left, return then to the centre and then to right;
3. Repeat in a rhythmical manner and gradually increase the range of motion.

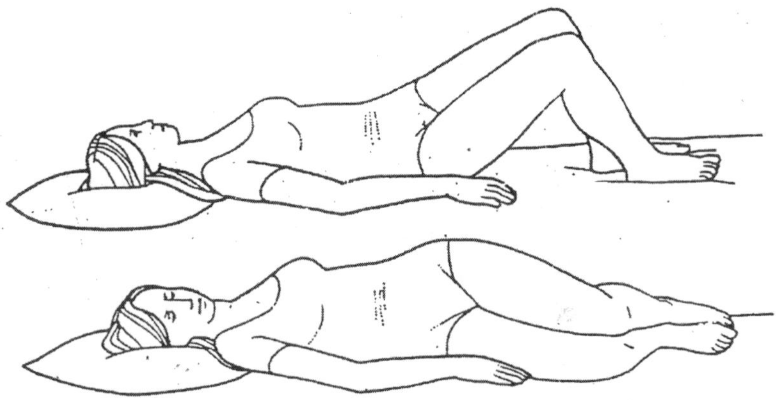

Exercise-III: Hip Updrawing/waist exercise

1. Lie on back with one leg bent and other leg straight;
2. Keep the bent leg still;
3. Make the straight leg shorten by drawing it up from hip and waist. Then make it longer by stretching down
4. Repeat with other leg bent.

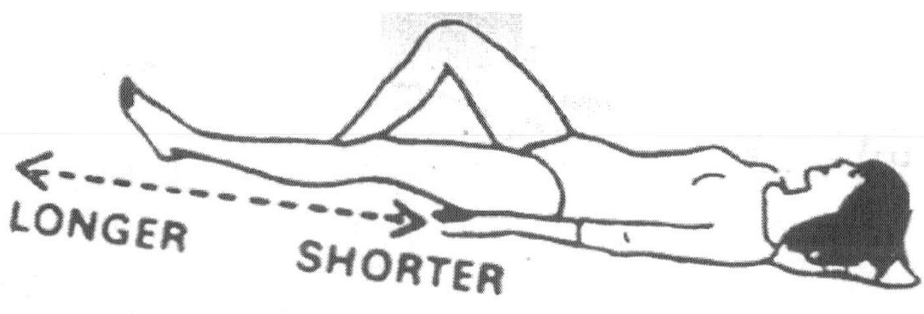

Exercise-IV: Pelvic floor

1. Lying, sitting or standing, tighten up between the legs as if trying very hard not to pass urine;
2. Hold for a count of 4, let go slowly;
3. Repeat 4 or 6 times, several times every day;
4. Do this at any time of day or night to ensure that pelvic floor muscles are supple and elastic, allows the baby's head to pass through easily.

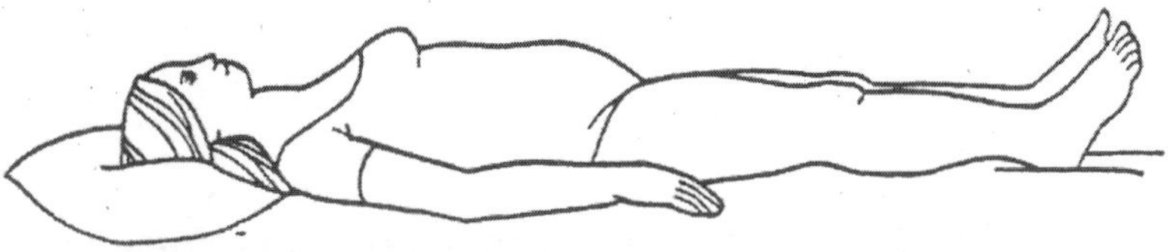

Exercise-V: Leg Rolling

1. Lie on back with legs straight
2. Keeping the shoulders flat, slowly and smoothly lift the left leg and keeping it straight, role it over to touch the right side of the bed and return it to starting position.
3. Repeat, using the right leg to touch the left side of the bed, relax
4. Begin with 2 repetitions, gradually progressing to 10.

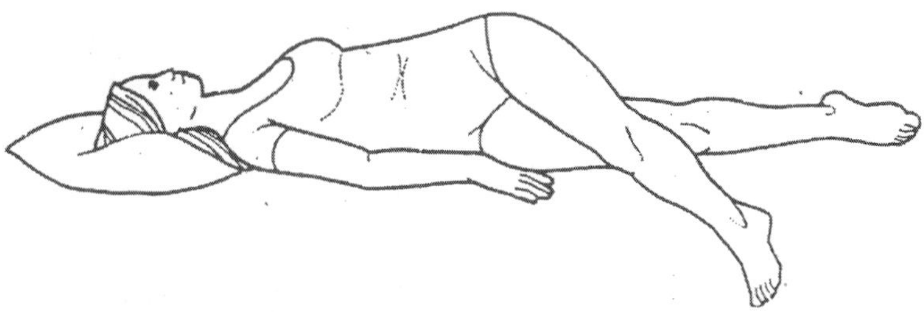

Chapter 9

Perinatal Care

Introduction

The transition from pregnancy to labour is a sequence of events that begins gradually. The first stage of labour; although difficult to diagnose, is usually recognized by the onset of regular uterine contraction and culminates in complete dilation of cervix.

This chapter aims at:

1. Define the term labour and describe the stages of labour;
2. Describe the onset of labour, its causes and diagnosis;
3. Describe the physiological changes that occur during labour;
4. Describe the measures for the evaluation of progress of labour;
5. Discuss the care of mother and assess the maternal and foetal wellbeing.

LABOUR

Labour is defined as the process by which the fetus, placenta and the membranes are expelled through the birth canal (Cassidy 1999).

Normal Labour

Labour is said to be normal when:

1. It occurs at term
2. Fetus presents by Vertex
3. Onset is spontanous
4. Completed within 18 hours
5. No complication occurs.

The Three P's of Normal Labour

The labour process involves a relationship between the "three P's" the Power or utermie contractions, the pelvis including size and shape, the passenger including size, position and presentation of fetus.

Factors Leading to Onset of Labour

1. Hormonal factors-oxytocin progesterone, oestrogen, prostaglandims
2. Pressure on cervix
3. Over distension of uterus
4. Others like febrile illness, eclampsia, fear and shock

Stages of Labour

Labour is divided into four stages.

First Stage

Is that of dilatation of cervix. It begins with regular rhythmic contractions ends with fully dilated cervix

Second Stage

Is that of expulsion. It begins with full dilatation of cervix and ends with the expulsion of the fetus.

Third Stage

Is that of expulsion of placenta and membranes. It starts with the birth of the baby and ends with the complete expulsion of the placenta and membrane.

Forth Stage

Is one hour following the expulsion of placenta and membranes.

Average Duration of Stages of Labour

	Ist Stage	*2nd Stage*	*3rd Stage*
Primi	13 hrs.	1 hr.	10 mts.
Multi	7.5 hrs.	30 mts.	10 mts.

Premonitory Signs of Labour

These are the signs and symptoms of impending labour:-

Lightening

Two to three weeks before the onset of labour, the lower uterine segment expands and allows the fetus to sink lower. With the descent of the foetus engagement occurs. The fundus no longer presses the diaphragm and woman can breath easily.

Cervical Changes

The cervix becomes soft and begins to efface and dilate slightly.

Show

With the softening and effacement of the cervix the cervical mucus plug (operculum) is expelled resulting in a small amount of blood loss from the exposed cervical capillaries. This blood stained mucus discharge is termed as bloody show.

Frequency of Micturation

Congestion of pelvis and pressure of gravid uterus leads to frequency of micturation.

Late Pregnancy Feeling

Some woman experience a sudden burst of energy and a compulsion to clean everything or rearrange household things. This is often referred to as nesting instinct.

Comparison of True and False Labour

True Labour	*False Labour*
1. Contractions occur regularly	Contractions are irregular
2. Contractions increase in frequency duration and intensity	Usually no change
3. Progressive effacement and dilatation of cervix	No increase in dilatation of cervix
4. Discomfort starts in the back and ache radiates around to abdomen	Not accompanied by back ache
5. Pain is not relieved by ambulation	May be relieved by ambulation
6. Show is usually present	Not present

Physiological Changes in the First Stage of Labour

Fundal Dominance

Each uterine contraction starts in the fundus near one of the Cornua and spreads across and downwards. Each contraction is longest and intense in fundus this pattern permits the cervix to dilate and fundus to expel the fetus.

Polarity

A neuromuscular harmony prevails between the two poles or segments of the uterus through out labour. The upper pole contracts stronger and retracts to expel the fetus the lower pole contracts slightly and dilates to allow expulsion to occur.

Contraction and Retraction

Contraction

Is a temporary shorting and thickening of muscle fibres.

Retraction

Is a permanent partial shortening of muscle fibres which has been in a state of contraction. In labour, the muscles of the upper segment contract and retract regularly, rhythmically and with increasing frequency, strength and duration. Each contraction has three phases-increment, acme and decrement.

Dilatation and Thinning of Lower Uterine Segment

The thickening and shortening of the upper segment achieves dilatation and thinning of the passive lower segment.

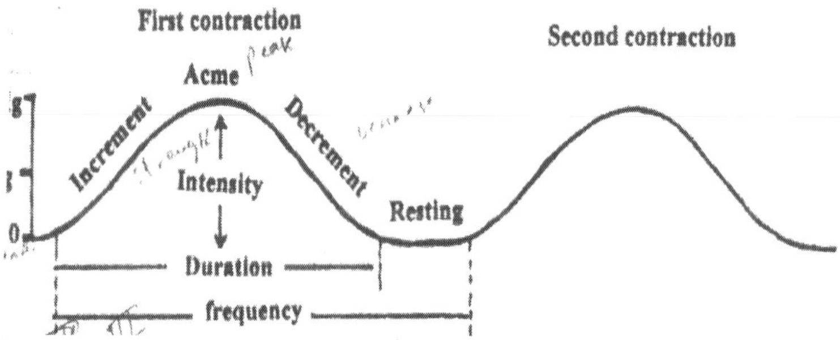

Characteristics of Uterine Contractions

Retraction Ring

With progressive Uterine contractions, the upper uterine segment becomes shorter and thicker and the lower uterine segment becomes thinner as it dilates. The Junctions of the two segments are known as retraction ring.

Cervical Effacement

It is the thinning of the cervix and the shortening of the cervical canal from its usual length of 2 to 3 cm to one, so it widens at the level of the internal os.

Show

As a result of the dilatation of cervix, the operculum is expelled. This may occur a few hours before or within few hours after labour starts.

Formation of Forewaters

As the lower uterine segment stretches the chorion becomes detached from it and the increased intra uterine pressure causes this sac of fluid to buldge through the dilated os. The bag of water seen in front of the well fitting head is called forewater and behind the hindwater.

Rupture of Membranes

Ideally the rupture of membranes (ROM) occurs at the end of first stage of labour when cervix is fully dilated and no longer supports the bag of forewaters. ROM may occur at any time during labour or even before labour starts.

Chapter 10

Care of Woman During First Stage of Labour

Admission to the Labour Unit

Welcome the labouring woman. This may be her first admission to hospital so carry out admission orders like changing hospital gown, safeguarding the personal belongings, etc.

History

Ask why she has come to the hospital, review history from the OPD card. Assess the woman for contractions, show, and rupture membranes.

Examination

1. Assess for general condition, note oedema, record pulse, blood pressure, test urine for sugar and protein.

2. Palpate abdomen gently and with warm hands, record fundal height, lie, presentation, position and level of head in fifths. Record duration and frequency of contractions.
3. Record fetal heart rate and inform about fetal and maternal condition
4. Vaginal examination to confirm and diagnose labour and assess progress of labour. Record all information in partogram.

Partogram

Is a single page graphic chart, designed to record all the important information about the woman and fetus during labour. The progress of labour is recorded as a simple graph with time on horizontal axis and the important features of labour on the vertical axis. All the observations such as BP, fetal heart, uterine contractions, findings of vaginal examination and head palpable in fifths are charted.

Promotion of Physical Wellbeing

The woman is allowed to ambulate if not centra indicated in bleeding, rupture of membranes, pregnancy induced hypertension, cardiac disease or any medical problem. Ambulation may decrease the need for analgesics, shortens labour and decreases incidence of fetal heart rate abnormalities.

1. Allow the mother to assume any comfortable position except dorsal recumbent which may result in supine hypotensive syndrome, leading to fetal distress.
2. Encourage deep breathing during contraction
3. Massage back if she complaints of back ache.

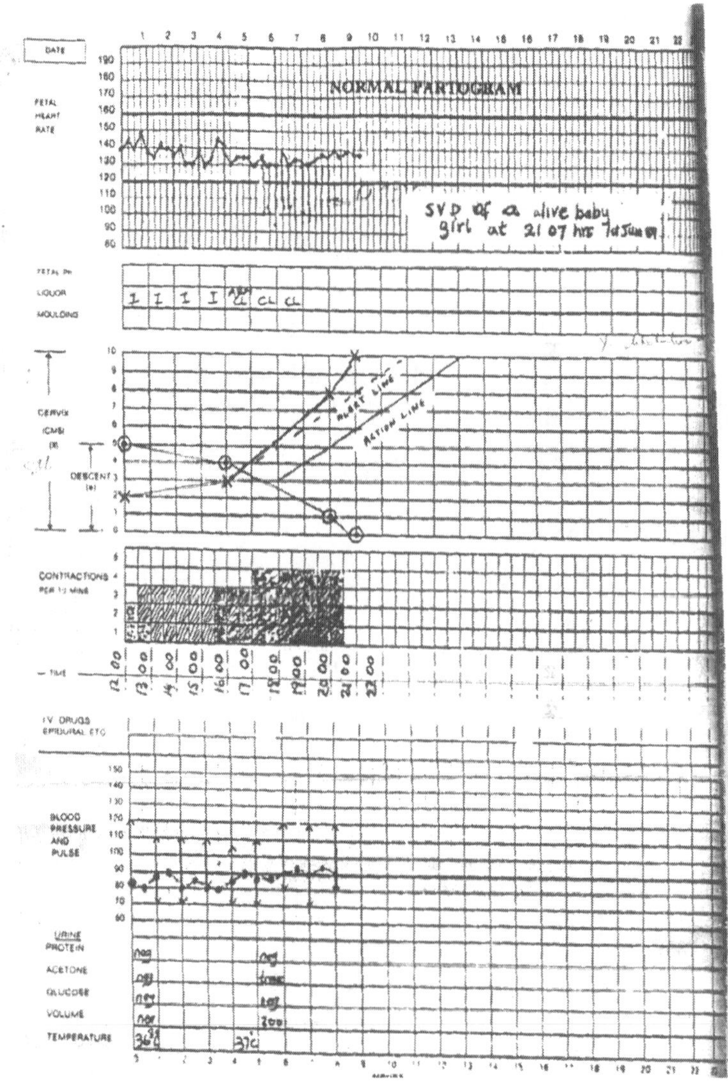

Partogram

4. Be with the woman, reassure her and encourage her to express her discomfort, fear and anxiety.
5. Change the pad in excessive veginal discharge.

Nutrition and Hydration

The woman's need for energy is met through nourishing give oral fluids at frequent intervals.

1. Solid foods are usually avoided since gastric emptying is prolonged during labour and also in anticipation of anaesthesia.
2. Sometimes I/V fluids may be given to provide energy and prevent dehydration.
3. If the mouth is dry provide mouth wash and sips of water.
4. Maintain intake and output chart

Bladder Care

To maintain empty bladder, the woman should be encouraged to pass urine every two to three hours during labour. The urine should be tested for the presence of glucose, ketones and proteins. A full bladder is associated with poor uterine contraction. It prevents descent of foetal head and can also cause injuries to bladder. Retention of urine frequently occurs in labour and catheterization may be required.

Observations

1. Reaction of woman to labour
2. Temperature every 4 hours
3. BP, Pulse, respiration every hour
4. Uterine contractions for frequency duration are checked every 30 mts.
5. If membranes are ruptured note the colour of liquor.

6. Assess progress of labour like descent of head per abdomen cervical dilatation and descent of head per vagina.

Enema

Enema stimulates uterine contractions, ensures a clean field without fecal contamination at the time of delivery. Soap and water enema is given in late-first stage or in rapid progressive labour.

Perineal Shave

The purpose is to prevent infection. Provides for cleanliness and easy viewing of the perinuctm.

Chapter 11
Second Stage of Labour

Introduction

The Second stage of labour is a time when the mother's passive control during the long hours of the first stage is replaced by intense physical effort and exertion for a comparatively short period. Both parents require stamina, courage and confidence in the skill of delivering baby.

This chapter aims at:

1. Explain the second stage of labour;
2. Describe the physiological changes during second stage of labour;
3. Discuss the care of mother during this stage.

Physiological Changes

Descend

Descend of fetal presenting part which begins during first stage of labour reached its maximum at the end of first stage of labour continues through second stage of labour.

Uterine Action

Contractions are strong, frequent and longer approximately every two minutes, lasting 60-90 seconds. The nature of contractions changes, become more expulsive as pressure is exerted on rectum and pelvic floor. Mother feels urge to push and the woman begins to voluntary beardown.

Rupture of Membrane

The membranes often rupture spontaneously at the second stage of labour. With the rupture of membranes the head flexion increases and progress of labour increases.

Dilatation and Gaping of Anus and Perenial Bulging

Deep engagement of presenting part and maternal pushing produce this sign during late second stage of labour.

Appearance of Presenting Part

Excessive moulding may result from prolonged labour in the formation of a large caput which may protrude through the cervix prior to full dilatation.

Congestion of the Vulva

If the second stage lasts longer than two hours in primigravida or one hour for multigravida is considered abnormal.

Care of Woman During Second Stage of Labour

Promotion of Comfort

1. Encourage mother to rest and let muscles relax in between contractions. Sips of water to provide moisture and relieve dryness of mouth. Keep the woman informed about progress.
2. Assist the woman in her pushing effort by propup with additional pillows to assume semi-recumbent position. Encourage her to relax between contractions and push during contractions.
3. Maternal and fetal monitoring every 15 mts.

Preparation of Delivery Room

Delivery room should always be ready for conduction of labour. Safety of the labouring mother should always be ensured. If the woman is transferred from one bed to another it should be between contractions, supporting the mother adequately. Provide enough privacy. Maintain strict asepsis in the conduction of labour. Make sure that room is warm enough for the baby. Ensure that the resuscitation trolley is ready for use.

Conduction of Labour

After being positioned for delivery, the perineum is cleaned and delivery is conducted under strict aseptic precautions.

Steps to be Observed During Delivery Process

Control

Control the head by flexing it as it is delivered to prevent pereneal laceration.

Cord

Check that the cord is not around the neck, if so and it is loose, it can be slipped over the head, if it is tight it should be clamped and cut.

Suckout

Suckout the baby's mouth and nose gently as soon as head is delivered.

Rotation

Wait for the natural rotation of the head.

Shoulders

Deliver the anterior shoulder first and then the posterior shoulder slowly.

Syntometrine

Give the mother IM syntometrine 1 ml when the baby's anterior shoulder is delivered or after the expulsion of placenta to stimulate contractions and to prevent bleeding.

Time

Note the time of birth.

Chapter 12

Immediate Care of the New Born

Introduction

The new born baby's survival is dependent on his ability to adapt to his extra uterine environment. Continued dependence on the mother for nutrition and safety necessitates the establishment of an emotional relationship which is initiated at the time of birth.

This Chapter Aim at:

1. Describe the physiological changes taking place at birth;
2. Discuss the care of the baby immediately after birth;
3. Identify normal characteristics of the newborn.

Initial Care

As the baby's head is born, excess mucus may be wiped gently from his mouth. Avoid touching the nares with suction. The time of birth and sex of the baby are noted and recorded once the baby is completely expelled.

Clearing the Airway

Most babies achieve a clear airway unaided. If necessary the airway can be cleared with the aid of mucus extract or soft suction catheter.

Clamping and Cutting the Cord

Clamping the umbilical cord is done by placing two instrument clamps on the cord about 8-10 cm from the umbilicus with enough room between them to allow for easy cutting of the cord. Application of a gauze swab over the cord while cutting it with scissors will prevent blood spraying the delivery field. The cord is usually clamped and cut immediately after birth. A plastic clamp is placed 2-3 cm from the umbilicus and excess cord is cut off. This clamp is disposable and can be removed when the cord has dried up.

APGAR Score

Healthy baby cries at birth within 20 seconds. In 1953 virginea Apgar USA introduced a scoring system to evaluate cardiac status of new born. When baby cries at birth Apgar score is 7-10. The score is assessed at 1 minute and 5 minutes after birth. Medical aid should be sought if the score is less than 7".

The APGAR Score

Sign	*Score*		
	0	*1*	*2*
Heart rate	Absent	Slow, less than 100	Fast, above 100
Respiratory effort	Absent	Slow, irregular	Good, Crying
Muscle tone	Limp of extremities	Some flexion	Active
Reflex irritability	No response	Grimace	Cry, Cough
Colour	Blue, pale	Body Pink extremities blue	Completely Pink

Total score: 10, Normal: 7-10,

Mild asphyxia: 4-6, Severe Asphyxia: 0-3.

Identification

It is very important to label the baby with the mother's name and registration number so that there is no mistake in identity. Bracelets must be placed around both ankles of the baby as well as of mother and checked on daily basis to see that they are still present these bracelets neither be too tight nor too loose and should remain on the baby until discharged from hospital.

Warmth

It is very important that the baby is kept warm at birth because he will loose heat and rapidly through evaporation. He should be dried gently and wrapped in a warm dry towel skin to skin contact with the mother, covering the baby's head, the provision of overhead radiant heaters within labour room helps to reduce hypothermia.

Birth Weight and Measurements

1. The baby is weighted as soon as possible after birth. The normal weight: 2500-4000 gm
2. Normal length: 44-55 cm
3. Crown rump length: 35 cm
4. Crown heel length: 51 cm
5. Chest circumference: 1-2 cm less than head circumference
6. These all are recorded in baby's notes, or mother's notes.

Examination

It is very important that the baby is examined properly to determine any abnormalities. So a head to toe examination is done as follows:

General Appearance

1. Body symmetry
2. Head large
3. Small hips
4. Protruding abdomen
5. Colour
6. Respiratory effort
7. Muscle tone
8. Temperature

Assessment of Head and Neck

Observe and palpate head for any moulding or caput succedaneum

1. Palpate fontanelles for fullness or depression

2. Ears–shape and position
3. Eye–size, shape, haemorrhage
4. Mouth–cleff lip/palate, tongue tie
5. Neck–length, webbing, mobility
6. Skin–abrasions, spots, pustules, birth marks
7. Nose–symmetry, septum, patency, flaring of nostrils.

Assessment of Body

1. Measurements of weight and length
2. General activity-posture, responsiveness
3. Skin-lanugo, vernix, texture, colour, rash, pigmentation meconuim staining

Thorax

1. Size, symmetry, shape
2. Breath sounds-respiratory rate
3. Heart sound-rhythm and rate
4. Breasts-engorgement

Abdomen

1. Shape
2. Umbilicus-cord vessels
3. Femoral pulses

Genitals

1. Appropriateness of sex
2. Female-labia, discharge
3. Male-urethral opening, scrotum testes
4. Urine-amount, colour

Back

1. Spine-vertebrae, symmetry
2. Anus-patency, meconuim

Extremities

1. Symmetry
2. Abnormalities
3. Movement
4. Digits-hands, feet, webbing
5. Hips-range of movement
6. Feet

Neurological Assessment

1. Rooting and sucking
2. Grasp reflex-palmer grasp reflex-hands, feet
3. Moro reflex- startle reflex-hold the baby with head supported, allow the head to drop back-lateral extension of arms, opening of hands
4. Stepping reflex-when held upright makes stepping movements.

Others

1. Check for presence of identity bands
2. Upon completion of examination baby should be given to the mother for breast feeding
3. Early feeding is recommended to prevent hypoglycaemia and to promote mother-infant bonding.

Chapter 13

Third Stage of Labour

Introduction

The focus of mother is on her newborn infant. There is a sense of emotional and physical relief.

This Chapter Aims at:-

1. Describe the mechanism of placental separation and normal haemostasis;
2. Enumerate the use of oxytocic drug in the third stage of labour;
3. Outline the Nursing Management of mother immediately after delivery of the placenta and membranes.

Physiological Changes

Placental Separation

Placental separation is the result of the abrupt decrease in size of uterine cavity following delivery of baby. The woman is observed for sign of placental separation like:

1. The uterus rises up in the abdomen and becomes round and hard.
2. The umbilical cord lengthens
3. A sudden gush of blood appears at the vulva.

Expulsion of the Placenta

Placental expulsion begins with the descend of the placenta into the lower uterine segment. Active management by controlled cord traction and use of oxytocic drugs is widely used as it reduces blood loss and shortens third stage.

Hemostasis

The normal volume of blood flow through the placental site is 500=800 ml per minute. This has to be arrested within seconds to prevent serous haemorrhage

Management

After expulsion of placenta and membranes, make sure that the uterus is well contracted:

1. Careful inspection of vagina, perineum are important to detect any lacerations
2. Examine the placenta and membranes for completeness, general appearance cord vessels and weight of placenta.

Chapter 14

Fourth Stage of Labour

Introduction

The fourth stage of labour is the stage of recovery. It is critical period for the mother and newborn. They not only recover from physical process of birth but also are initiating new relationships.

This Chapter Aims at:

1. Explain the physiological changes during fourth stage of labour;
2. Describe the nursing care during 4th stage of labour;
3. Describe the observations to be done on the mother.

Physiological Changes

The delivered mother should remain in the delivery room for at least one hour following delivery. Most of this time will be spent in clearing up and completing records but careful observation of the mother and baby is very important.

Assess the following physiologic status:

1. Maternal vital signs
2. Uterine contractility
3. Lochia
4. Bladder status
5. Perneal conditions

Observations

1. The vital signs checked and recorded every 15 mts.
2. The fundus should be checked on several occasions to ensure that it remains well contracted and prevent bleeding.
3. Lochia should be observed for flow, colour and consistency.
4. Perineum is inspected for edema and heamotoma formation.

Bladder

Bladder is kept empty because it will prevent the uterus for contracting properly. A full bladder cause uterine atony and severe post partum bleeding. Mother is encouraged to pass urine.

Personal Hygiene

Most mothers appreciate a wash and change of clothes after delivery. Attention should be paid to perenial toilet and a clean pad applied.

Nutrition

A drink is usually appreciated and if the mother is hungry she should be given a light snack.

Breast Feeding

Most mothers wish to put their baby to the breast as soon as possible. The baby is usually very alert at this time and sucking reflex is strong. The baby is observed for the security of cord clamp, observe skin colour respiration and temperature.

Records

Records for mother and baby should be completed during this time.

Transfer

Before the mother is transferred to the postnatal ward, the fundus and lochia must be checked.

Chapter 15

Care of the Woman after Delivery

Admission

To postnatal ward-welcome the mother, observe her general condition, palpate uterus and observe lochia check for emptying of bladder.

Rest and Sleep

Mother should have sufficient rest and sleep. Inability to sleep other than due to feeding the baby may be an early sign of puerperal neurosis.

Ambulation

The mother should be encouraged to mobilise from about 6 hours after delivery. This helps to reduce thrombo–embolic disorders.

Nutrition

Attention and education must be paid to the kind of food that she eats, so that she maintains her own health and lactates adequately. She should have a well balanced diet with adequate protein and fluid intake.

Hygiene

Her first shower after delivery should be supervised in case she feels dizzy or unwell. She should be instructed for the use of the bidet and encourage to use it as often as possible. When attending to her personal hygiene, perineal pads should be changed frequently and the perineum kept clean and dry to promote healing.

Micturation

There will be a marked diuresis for 2-3 days following delivery. The bladder should be emptied as soon as possible after delivery. Numbness due to injury or pressure during delivery makes the woman unware of a full bladder.

Bowels

The bowel probably was emptied during labour so there may be no bowel action for a couple of days. Painful perineum or haemorrhoids may restrict bowel action.

Breast Feeding

The first feed should be given as soon as possible after birth, as the baby is alert and sucks well at birth. The baby should be fed on demand and there should be no limit to the length of time that he sucks. Breast feeding should be happy and satisfying experience of the mother and her baby.

Postnatal Exercises

Postnatal exercises help to give the mother a sense of wellbeing, encourage good circulation and restore the muscle tone of the abdominal wall and pelvic floor. Emphasise the need for regular exercises.

Haemoglobin

This is checked in the second day after delivery and the mother treated accordingly.

Discharge

Before leaving the hospital the mother and baby are examined by the doctor. The mother may be given iron tablets to take and the reason and importance for taking them should be carefully explained to her.

Psychology of the Puerperuim

Major emotional changes take place in the majority of woman during the puerperuim. It takes 6-12 weeks for a woman to return to her normal emotional state. During first few days the woman is normally in a state of euphoria, excitement and restlessness. For 3rd day the "bules" may occur at any time. This is a normal reaction to childbirth and most mothers have recovered within 24 hours.

Self Care Activities

1. Normal involution
2. General hygiene
3. Perineal care
4. Breast care (support, cleansing comfort measures, milk expression)
5. Nutrition and hydration

6. Rest and sleep
7. Postnatal exercises
8. Bowel and bladder elimination
9. Resuming sexual relationship and use of birth spacing methods
10. Infant care

Abnormal Signs to be Reported Like

1. Heavy vaginal bleeding; fever,
2. Foul smelling vaginal discharge;
3. Swollen, tender, red warm area on breast
4. Burning micturation
5. Persistent pelvic pain

Expected Outcome After Birth (Post Partum Period)

Expected outcome for physiological needs are:

1. The woman remains free from infection.
2. Demonstrate normal involution and lochia characteristics
3. Remains comfortable and injury free.
4. Demonstrate normal bowel and bladder patterns
5. Protect the health for future pregnancies and child birth
6. Integrate the new born into the family.
7. Demonstrate knowledge of breast care for breast feeding as appropriate.

Chapter 16

Postnatal Care

Introduction

Effective postnatal care is vital component of the puerperum. This chapter will concentrate on the normal physiological adaptation and management.

The processes of pregnancy reversed. This period is also called as fourth trimester of pregnancy.

This Chapter Aims at:

1. Describe the physiological changes of the puerperium;
2. Identify postnatal tasks;
3. Describe the care of the woman during puerperium.

Physiology and Management of Puerperium

The puerperium is a period of 6 weeks which begins as soon as the placenta is expelled. During this period a number is physiological changes takes place:

1. The reproductive organs return to the nonpregnant state (Involution).
2. The physiological changes in other systems of body, which occur during pregnancy, are reversed.
3. The secretion of milk in the breasts is initiated.

Duration

The puerperium (Postnatal period) is divided into immediate (the first 24 hrs), early (upto 7 days) and remote up to the six weeks.

Involution of Uterus

The term involution means return of the uterus to its normal size, tone and position. The vagina, ligaments of uterus and the pelvic floor also return to their pre-pregnant state. During the process of involution the lining of the uterus is cast off in the lochia. The rate of involution can be measured by the rate of descent of the uterine fundus. On the first day the height above the symphysis pubis is about 12 cm, there is a steady decrease in the height of uterus of about I cm a day. Careful palpation of the uterus and observation of lochia reveals whether involution progresses normally.

Lochia

The lochia is the discharge from the uterus occurring after child-birth and persists for first 3-4 weeks of the puerperium. Lochia are described in three stages:

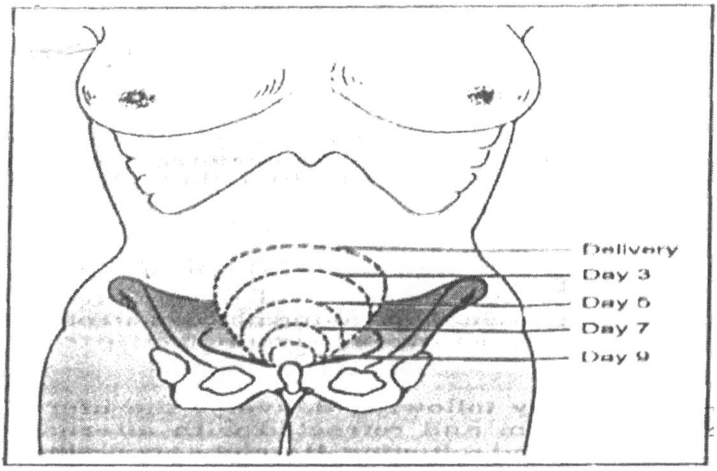

Fundal Height and Uterine Involution

Red Lochia (Lochia Rubra)

Lasts for the first 3-4 days. It is usually red blood in colour and contains primarily blood and decidual tissue.

Serous Lochia (Lochia Serosa)

Is paler than rubra and is serous and pink as at contains less blood but mere serum. It lasts for 5-9 days.

White Lochia (Lochia Alba)

Is the last lochia. It is pale, creamy white and consists leukocytes, decidual cells and mucus and may continue for a further 2-3 weeks.

Overies and Uterine Tubes

Becomes pelvic organs again.

Breasts

Lactation is initiated by the secretion of prolactin by the anterior pituitary gland. The secretion from the breasts is called colostrum which starts during pregnancy but becomes abundant during this period. The milk comes into the breasts about the third day after delivery.

Change in Other Systems

Urinary Tract

There is marked diuresis after delivery which lasts for 2-3 days.

Alimentary Tract

Progesterone level falls, so heart burn improves and constipation may continue for a few days.

Circulatory System

Blood volume decreases.

Endocrine System

Ocstrogen and progesterone levels falls.

Musculo Skeletal System

The softened pelvic joints and ligaments during pregnancy gradually return to normal over about 3 months, abdominal and pelvic floor muscles regain their tone with the help of exercises.

Postnatal Care Tasks

Bonding

To assist the bonding between the mother and the baby.

Breast Feeding

To establish breast feeding.

Birth Spacing

To advise the mother about importance of natural birth spacing by breast feeding.

Health Education

To give advice on the care of the mother and her nutrition, care of the baby, cleanliness, feeding, immunisation and warmth.

Chapter 17

Home Birth

Home birth takes into account the woman's and her family's personal and social circumstances which influence the health and wellbeing of her and her baby. It promotes the wellbeing of mothers and babies and support sound parenting and stable families.

This Chapter Aims at:

1. Describe the role of Midwife in home birth;
2. Reviews the skills a Midwife requires for home birth;
3. Describe the process, equipment required for birth at home;
4. Identifies the care given during birth at home.

Home birth is the birth of baby in the family home. This usually occurs because the parents believe that birth is a natural process and want to take place within the environment of the family home. This is known as planned home birth. Sometimes babies are born at home unexpectedly because labour begins prematurely or precipitously. This is known as unplanned home birth or born before arrival ((BBA).

Home birth is the another alternative to traditional hospital delivery. Parents who have participated in home delivery find that it is a warm, close, loving experience for which they have responsibility and control, the newborn infant is immediately incorporated into the family and there is a continuous contact between the new born and his family which facilitates bonding process and establish a family unit.

Care of the Woman at Home

Preparation of the Family

1. Discuss the advantages and disadvantages of home birth, try to provide as much as factual information as possible.
2. Explain the role of the midwife during a home birth and conduction of labour.
3. Explain how to contact Midwife when woman is in labour.

The Mother

1. Discuss pain relief
2. Comfort aids for labour

3. A suit case packed in case of transfer to hospital considering transport and communication.
4. Arrangement for the care and preparation of any other children
5. Ideally mother/adult woman should be available to care the children.

The Baby

1. Cot, baby clothes
2. Nappies-warm hat
3. Hot warm bottle (to warm cot)

The Room

1. Protection for pillows mattress and carpet like polythene covers and old sheets spared bed linen)
2. Reliable heating and lighting
3. Clean surface
4. Bathroom or other washing facilities with soap and towel

Equipments

1. Maternity pack containing cotton wool balls, sanitary pads and vaginal examination pack.
2. Midwifery delivery bag containing the following equipments:
   - Pinard stethoscope
   - Sphygnomenometer
   - Urine testing equipment
   - O_2 in small cylinder for baby by face mask
   - Disposable suction apparatus

- Intravenous set and fluids
- Plastic bags for clinical wastes
- Sterile gloves with K.Y. Jelly
- Amni hook (toothed forceps)
- Glycerine suppositories or disposable phosphate enema
- Urethral catheters

Delivery pack

1. Two artery ferceps
2. Cord scissor
3. Episiotomy scissors
4. Card clamps
5. Suture pack
6. Stitch scissor
7. Needle holder
8. Forceps
9. Suture material
10. Lignocani cain 10 per cent
11. 20 ml syringe and needles

Maternal Drugs

1. Syntometrin 1 ml
2. Ergometrin 05 mg
3. Analgesic drugs (pathidin)

Baby Equipments

1. Laryngoscope (baby size)
2. Baby ambubag

3. Endo tracheal tubes
4. Baby drugs like nalaxone

Conduction of Labour at Home

Conduction of labour is similar as in hospital. In case of any complications she is transferred early to nearest PHC.

Procedure

1. Check the kit and get it completed before procedure
2. Greet the mother and her relatives
3. Keep the kit at a safe place near the mother
4. Ask the relatives to keep water boiling
5. Open the kit and takeout swabs, gloves, rubber catheter and instruments to boil
6. Make her lie down on prepared bed
7. Assess progress of labour
8. Check fetal heart by fetoscope/stethoscope
9. Shave the vulva/perineum if necessary
10. Observe leakage or bleeding for complications
11. Give enema to empty bladder and stimulate uterine contractions
12. Take out the boiled equipments with chettle forcep
13. Take out the boiled swabs in a bowl
14. Pour dettol lotion on sterile swabs
15. Keep the sterile articles in plastic sheet near the woman
16. Place the woman in dorsal position
17. Spread mackintosh/plastic sheet under the hips of the mother

18. Keep dustbin/pot under the bed
19. Put on plastic apron, scrub the hands for five minutes with soap and water
20. Wear the gloves
21. Clean the vulva and perineal area with swabs from upward to downward using one stroke only
22. Encourage her to bear down when OS is fully dilated
23. Give oral fluids to keep her hydrated
24. Support perineum to prevent tear
25. Keep one pad over the rectum if she is passing motion to prevent infection.
26. Place the palm of left hand on the advancing head and fingers pointing to sinciput to control sudden expulsion of fetus.
27. When crowing takes place ask mother to stop pushing to prevent tear or laceration
28. Spread the fingers over the vertex
29. Feel if cord is around the neck
30. Clamp and cut the cord if around neck to prevent asphyxia
31. Clean the eyes, mouth, nostrils of the baby.
32. Conduct delivery of the body and drain secretions from mouth and nostrils
33. Note time of delivery
34. Make the baby to cry by taping the back
35. Clamp and cut the cord
36. Clean the baby and observe for apgar scoring and handover to relatives

37. Observe for signs of separation of placenta
38. Deliver placenta
39. Examine placenta and membranes
40. Administer inj. Mathergin I/M
41. Clean the mother and apply sutures if episiotomy
42. Apply pads and give comfortable position
43. Offer a hot drink
44. Tie the cord of the baby, take weight, observe for congenital abnormalities
45. Clean and wear clothes

After Care

Remove all the articles; wash the instruments, bowls and kidney tray etc.

Dry all articles and pack them in kit.

Put all the dirty wastes like placenta, swabs in the dust bin/plastic bag and handover to relatives to buried it.

Inform in case of any complaints.

Chapter 18

Postnatal Exercises

However busy you are, do make time to take care of your figure. A good figure is important for your health and confidence.

Exercise-I: To Tone Up the Tummy

1. Head on Pillow, Knees bent, Feet flat;
2. Put hands half way down your tummy;
3. Breath in feel your tummy go up;
4. Breath out completely;
5. Pull your tummy wall towards your back to squeeze out as much air as you can.

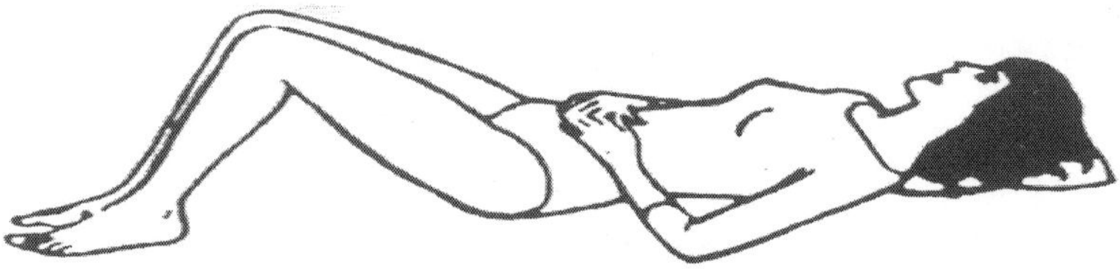

Exercise-II: Tone Up legs

1. Head on pillow, legs straight
2. Press back of knees and thighs downwards onto bed or floor
3. Relax.

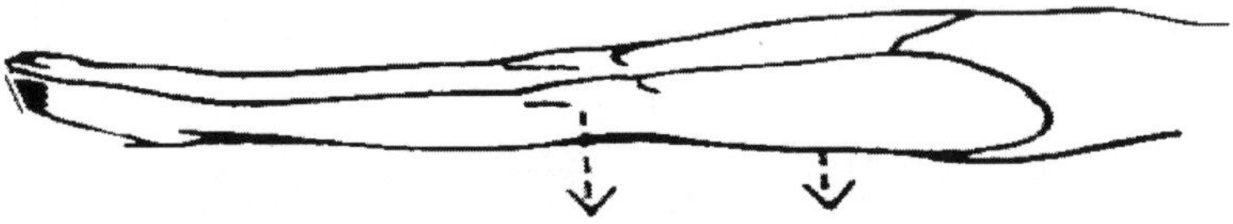

Exercise-III: For Tummy

1. Head on pillow, knees bent, feet flat
2. Tighten tummy muscles and pull in;
3. Press waist downwards, hard, to round spine;
4. Keep waist in contact with bed or floor.

   Lift the hips off it slightly by contracting your buttocks, relax.

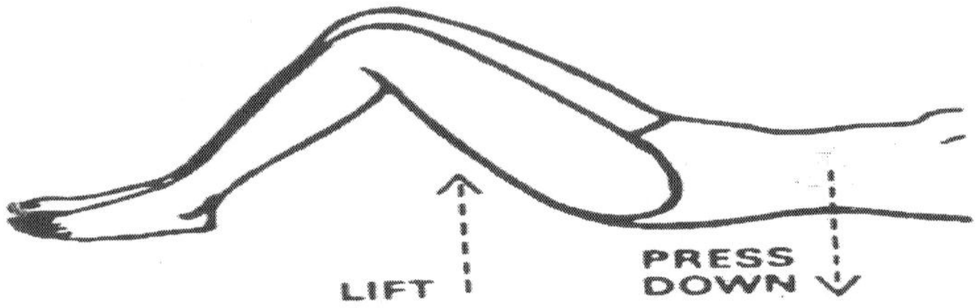

Exercise-IV: For Waist and Hips

1. Head on pillow, knees bent, arms stretched out side ways
2. Keep feet and shoulders still, knees together

3. Twisting from waist, swing both knees to touch bed or floor on left, while right hip turns towards ceiling;
4. Then swing knees over to touch on right, while left hip turns towards ceiling.

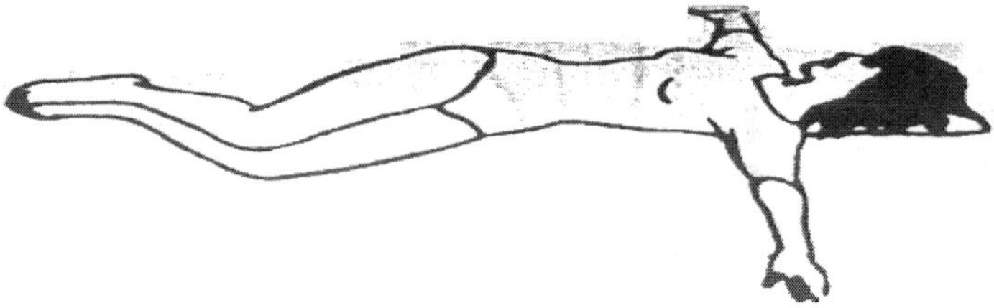

Exercise-V: For Back

1. Face down on floor, arms behind back;
2. Lift head and shoulders off floor, then lower and relax;
3. (If chest is uncomfortable, put one or two pillows under tummy)

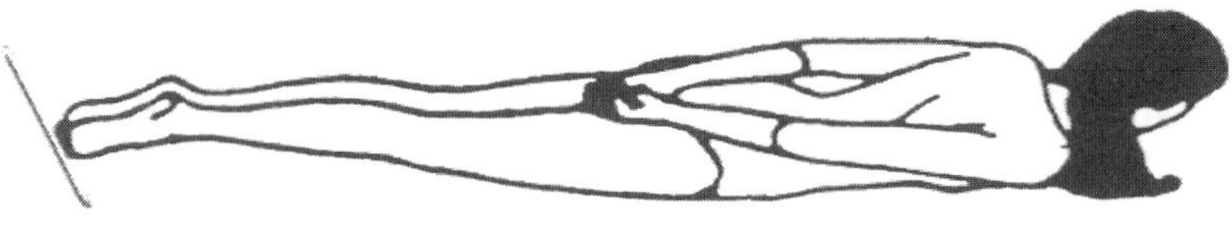

Exercise-VI: For Back

1. Face down on floor, forehead on hands;
2. Lift one leg behind, you, from the hips;
3. Keep it straight;
4. Lift as high as you can, without bending knees or turning body;

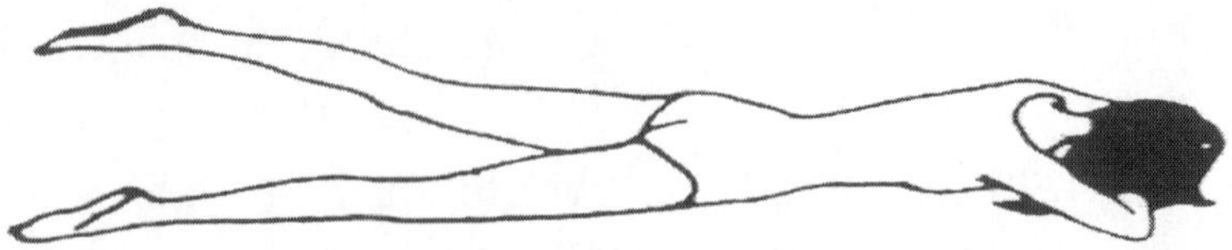

5. Lower it again;
6. Then lift the other leg, lower it again.

Bibliography

Bobak, Lowdermilk Maternity Nursing, 4th edition, Mosby, St. Louis Missouri, 1991.

Bennett, Ruth. Myles Textbook for Midwives, 13th edition, Churchill Livingstone, New York.

Dawn, C.S. Text Book of Obstetrics and Neonatology, 16th edition, Dawn Books, Kolkata, 2003.

Dutta, D.C., Textbook of Obstetrics' 5th edition. New Central Book Agency, Kolkata, 2001.

Freidman, E.A. Labour, Clinical Evaluation and Management 2nd Edition, Meridith, New York, 1978.

Indrani, T.K. Text Book of Midwifery, Jaypee Brothers, Medical Publishers, New Delhi, 2003.

Jacob Annamma. A Comprehensive Text Book of Midwifery, Jaypee Brothers, Medical Publishers, New Delhi, 2005.

Levy, V. Moore. The Midwife's Management of the third stage of Labour Nursing Times, pp. 47-50, 1985.

Park, K. Text Book of Preventive and Social Medicine, 16th Edition. Banarsidas Bhanut Publishers. Jabalpur 2000.

Royal College of Midwives-successful Breast Feeding, 2nd edition, Churchill Livingstone Edinburge, London, 1991.

Varney, Helen. Nurse-midwifery, 2nd Edition, Jones and Barlett Publishers-Boston 1996.

Index